Practical
to Learning
Difficulties

This book is dedicated to Francesca Gray

An A to Z
Practical Guide
to Learning
Difficulties

HARRY AYERS

 David Fulton Publishers

David Fulton Publishers Ltd
The Chiswick Centre, 414 Chiswick High Road, London W4 5TF

www.fultonpublishers.co.uk
www.onestopeducation.co.uk

David Fulton Publishers is a division of Granada Learning Limited, part of ITV plc.

British Library Cataloguing in Publication Data
A catalogue record for this book is available from the British Library.

ISBN: 1 84312 266 9

Reprinted 2006
10 9 8 7 6 5 4 3 2

Typeset by RefineCatch Ltd, Bungay Suffolk
Printed and bound in Great Britain

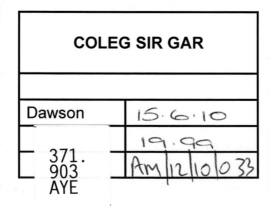

Preface

This book is intended as a useful and practical A to Z guide to learning difficulties and associated terms for a wide range of different readers including teachers, teaching assistants, mentors, social workers, educational social workers, care staff, counsellors, educational psychologists, students, parents, carers, voluntary workers and the general reader. The guide focuses on the learning difficulties of children and adolescents. The A to Z format is intended to make the guide accessible and user-friendly. This book is also intended to be a companion volume to *An A to Z Practical Guide to Emotional and Behavioural Difficulties* by Harry Ayers and Cesia Prytys, also published by David Fulton Publishers. This is useful in relation to learning difficulties because of the connections between EBD and learning difficulties.

This A to Z guide, for reasons of space, practicality and intended readership, has to be selective in terms of its entries. Many of the entries, but not all, have been selected on the basis of their common or relatively common occurrence and their practical usefulness to practitioners. Entries have been kept as succinct as possible but at the same time the aim has been to provide information about theories, approaches and interventions rather than simply defining terms.

The focus therefore has not only been on the definition and explanation of terms relating to learning difficulties but also, where appropriate, on different perspectives, approaches, treatments, interventions and strategies. An attempt has been made to recognise that controversies and conflicts exist in connection with certain terms while at the same time presenting some of the different perspectives on these controversies.

Every effort has been made to make the guide as up-to-date and as accurate as access to recent literature and information allows. The guide also, where appropriate, provides addresses, websites and phone numbers of supportive organisations. Selected references and bibliography are located underneath the entries, but for reasons of space these have been kept to a minimum. There is however a general bibliography at the back of the guide.

Ayers, H. and Prytys, C. (2002) *An A to Z Practical Guide to Emotional and Behavioural Difficulties*. London: David Fulton Publishers.

A

ABC

The letters ABC stand for antecedents, behaviour and consequences. The ABC is a method for recording specific, overt and observable behaviours. It is a method based on behavioural psychology. An ABC identifies the antecedents and consequences of specific and overt target behaviours. Antecedents are observable events occurring immediately before the target behaviour, and consequences are events occurring immediately afterwards. The target behaviour can be any behaviour such as that manifested in EBD or LD. It forms the basis for a functional analysis of behaviour.

Antecedents	Behaviour	Consequences
Teacher speaks negatively to child about her writing.	Child stops writing.	Child fails to finish written work.

Herbert, M. (1998) *Clinical Social Psychology* (2nd edn). Chichester: Wiley.
Sturmey, P. (1966) *Functional Analysis in Clinical Psychology*. Chichester: Wiley.

Absence

Poor attendance, avoidable and unavoidable, may become a contributory factor to learning difficulties. Absenteeism may be due to in-school factors such as negative teacher–student relationships or difficulties in coping with particular subjects. Out-of-school factors such as health problems, e.g. asthma and *petit mal* epilepsy, or psychosomatic illnesses, e.g. stomach upsets and headaches, or certain physical disabilities, may affect attendance. In particular absenteeism can affect hierarchical and sequential subjects such as foreign languages and mathematics. Additionally, absences can also affect test and examination results, undermining a pupil's self-confidence and motivation. To counteract the effects of absenteeism, interventions such as peer tutoring and the provision of missed work should be implemented. Follow-up is essential.

Absences (*petit mal*)

A type of epilepsy known as *petit mal*. These attacks originate in early childhood and are short-lived. The pupil looks dazed and ceases activity for a short period of time, then resumes activity. Episodes of *petit mal* can occur many times a day unless treated. Attacks may continue into adolescence and adulthood. If attacks are left untreated then learning and educational achievement can be adversely affected.

Academic skills disorders

Disorders of childhood characterised by impairment in academic skills within the school context. Specific types include developmental, arithmetical, and expressive writing and reading disorders.

Achievement

There are various aspects to achievement, including age and levels of achievement, motivation to achieve and achievement testing. Achievement age refers to the age at which, on average, pupils achieve a given level of performance and is used when age norms have been determined. Levels of achievement refer to the levels achieved through standardised tests. Motivation to achieve is the degree to which a pupil wishes to, strives to or makes an effort to attain a particular learning target or goal. Achievement tests measure a pupil's current or existing levels of skill or knowledge. There may exist a discrepancy between potential achievement and actual achievement. Judgements about potential achievement are usually based on IQ or cognitive ability tests.

ADD/ADHD

ADD stands for Attention Deficit Disorder and ADHD stands for Attention Deficit Hyperactivity Disorder. This disorder is believed to have a genetic and neurological basis and is described as a condition where the child or pupil experiences severe difficulties in maintaining attention or concentration, difficulties with impulse control and difficulties in controlling motor activity. The child or student is restless, talkative, often off-task, easily distracted and frequently fails to complete set tasks, and tasks that are finished are often of poor quality. The child or student fails to adhere to home and family routines and fails to meet parental and teacher expectations. Diagnosis of ADHD is through the observation of behaviour using criteria described in the DSM-IV (Diagnostic and Statistical Manual of Mental Disorders (4th edn 1994)). Psychiatrists or physicians usually diagnose the disorder. Three types are listed. It should be mentioned that there is a continuing debate, even controversy, over the nature, cause and prevalence of ADD/ADHD. In fact, currently there is no physical test, i.e. there is no existing biological or medical test for the disorder. A number of different behavioural assessment methods are used including teacher and parent rating scales and direct observation. Treatment for the disorder is primarily through medication. However, behavioural methods (operant techniques) and educational methods are also used to treat the disorder. The medication or drug used is a psycho-stimulant that is believed to stimulate the production of neurotransmitters that facilitate the transmission of information which, in turn, improve attention span, control impulsivity and reduce excessive motor activity. Those most often prescribed are Ritalin, Dexedrine, Cylert and Adderall. Psycho-stimulants can have side effects, e.g. insomnia or loss of appetite. These side effects are usually temporary. However, a rebound effect can occur in the evening when the effects of the drug diminish. Other treatments that have been suggested include the removal of food additives and the treatment of allergies. Teaching methods for increasing attention include placing the pupil at the front of the class, keeping the pupil away from distracting stimuli or situations, sitting the pupil away from problem pupils and sitting them by positive role models. Further methods include implementing simple, structured routines, prompting the pupil, using audio-visual aids and introducing novelty into lessons. Teaching methods for controlling impulsivity and hyperactivity include providing short tasks and encouraging controlled, purposeful movement.

Alban-Metcalfe, J. and Alban-Metcalfe J. (2001) *Managing Attention Deficit/Hyperactivity Disorder in the Inclusive Classroom*. London: David Fulton Publishers.

American Psychiatric Association (1994) *Diagnostic and Statistical Manual of Mental Disorders* (4th edn) (DSM-IV). Washington, DC: APA.

Cooper, P. and Bilton K.M. (2002) *Attention Deficit/Hyperactivity Disorder: A Practical Guide for Teachers* (2nd edn). London: David Fulton Publishers.

DuPaul, G.J. and Stoner, G. (1994) *ADHD in Schools: Assessment and Intervention Strategies*. New York: Guilford Press.

Hinshaw, S.P. (1994) *Attention Deficits and Hyperactivity in Children*. Thousand Oaks, CA: Sage.

Jones, G. (2002) *Educational Provision for Children with Autism and Asperger Syndrome*. London: David Fulton Publishers.

Kewley, G.D. (2001) *Attention Deficit Hyperactivity Disorder: Recognition, Reality and Resolution*. London: David Fulton Publishers.

World Health Organisation (1992). *International Classification of Diseases* (ICD-10).

Contact

ADHD Information Services, 10 Station Road, London NW7 2JU. Tel: 020 8906 9068; Fax: 020 8959 0727; e-mail: info@addiss.co.uk; www.addiss.co.uk;

Adolescents with learning difficulties

Such persons face particular problems on moving into secondary education as they often experience continuing difficulties within the areas of literacy and numeracy and also face the increasing demands of the National Curriculum. They need to adapt to different subject teachers, their teachers' personalities and different teaching styles and methods. If there is streaming or setting they frequently find themselves in the bottom streams or lowest sets and may experience a sense of failure or stigma. They may experience emotional and behavioural problems as a result of the transition to secondary education and as a result of increased curricular demands. Their absenteeism may increase due to the in-school factors mentioned above and also due to growing feelings of failure leading to avoidance or escape from the classroom and school context. Subject teachers may not feel trained or experienced enough to cope with adolescents with learning difficulties. Teachers may provide undifferentiated lessons that further increase their pupils' difficulties in accessing the curriculum. Many adolescents with learning difficulties are passive learners and develop an attitude called 'learned helplessness'. They tend to wait passively for help rather than attempt a task on their own. Often they lack confidence in their ability to learn and succeed. They also experience problems in attending to teachers, in accessing instructional materials and in being on task for long periods. They tend to give up easily, and even when they do experience success they tend to attribute that success to external factors such as luck or easy work.

Lerner, J. (2003) *Learning Disabilities* (9th edn). Boston, MA: Houghton Mifflin.

Affective factors

Anxiety and depression are just two affective factors that contribute to learning difficulties or are the result of learning difficulties. The impact of persistent failure can adversely affect a pupil's self-esteem, confidence, perceived self-efficacy, attitude and motivation. When confronted by certain tasks pupils may develop anxious feelings, fearing they will fail. This in turn may lead them to avoid or escape situations that elicit those feelings. Anxious feelings may also lead pupils to become aggressive and disruptive so as to disguise or cope with feelings of inadequacy and failure. They may develop learned helplessness. These feelings may, in themselves, inhibit learning through reducing attention span, decreasing levels of concentration and also interfering with working memory. Over a period of time, pupils may become depressed and develop feelings of low self-worth. This in turn reduces motivation. Pupils can become preoccupied with feelings of low self-esteem and hopelessness and give up making efforts to learn, to attend certain lessons or even to attend school. Pupils may in certain cases require counselling or therapy to treat their anxiety or depression. There are different types of counselling or therapy that can be used including behavioural, cognitive-behavioural, person-centred and psychodynamic approaches. In certain cases biologically based treatment may be prescribed in the form of medication.

Agraphia

A condition caused by brain damage and characterised by the loss or impairment of the ability to write. There are different types, i.e. aphasic and non-aphasic agraphias.

Alexia

A disability where there is a partial or total inability to recognise printed words. There is no loss or inadequacy of vision and no loss of recognition of the spoken word. It is sometimes called 'word-blindness'. It is an acquired inability to comprehend written or printed text.

Anxiety

Anxiety can adversely affect learning. Anxious pupils, with or without learning difficulties, may refuse to attempt tasks, avoid tasks altogether, fail to complete tasks or give up easily. Anxiety can affect short-term memory and concentration. In particular, some pupils have an aversion to, or severe anxiety regarding, mathematics. In some cases this amounts to a maths phobia. Anxiety can be due to other factors such as separation anxiety or a school phobia that adversely affects attendance at school.

Craig, K.D. and Dobson, K.S. (eds) (1995) *Anxiety and Depression in Adults and Children.* Thousand Oaks, CA: Sage.

Aphasia

A severe form of language impairment or lack of language skills, that is an inability to use or understand spoken language. Aphasia is due to brain injury or lesions. There is a variety of different types, e.g. anomic, ataxic, auditory, Broca's, conductive, developmental, global, optic, syntactic and Wernicke's.

Apraxia

Impairment in the ability to perform voluntary movements. This impairment is due to a lesion. As with aphasia there are various types including amnesic, constructional, ideational, ideokinetic and ideomotor.

Asperger, or Asperger's, syndrome

Asperger syndrome is a higher-functioning form of autism. There is a debate over the diagnostic criteria for the syndrome. It has been suggested that both autism and Asperger syndrome lie along the same continuum. The syndrome encompasses the social and behavioural elements of autism but is not characterised by cognitive and language deficits. In fact those manifesting the syndrome tend to have extended vocabularies. In older children it can be characterised by a very narrow range of interests and precocious skills such as arithmetical calculations, memorising lists, and advanced musical and artistic skills. It is believed to have a predominantly genetic basis.

Cumine, V., Leach, J. and Stevenson, G. (1998) *Asperger Syndrome: A Practical Guide for Teachers.* London: David Fulton Publishers.

Howlin, P. (1998) *Children with Autism and Asperger Syndrome: A Guide for Practitioners and Carers.* Chichester: Wiley.

Contact

The National Autistic Society, 393 City Road, London EC1 1NG. Tel: 020 7833 2299; Fax: 020 7833 9666; e-mail: nas@nasorg.uk; www.oneworld.org /autism-uk/

Assessment

There are various methods of assessing learning difficulties including standardised tests (norm- and criterion-referenced), task analysis, analysis of work examples, analysis of learning styles, curriculum-based measurement, diagnostic, dynamic and functional-behavioural assessment (see under separate entries). With regard to SEN assessment this refers to Statutory Assessment. This is a procedure undertaken by an LEA that may lead to a Statement of Special Educational Needs.

Galloway, D., Armstrong, D. and Tomlinson, S. (1994) *The Assessment of Special Educational Needs: Whose Problem?* London: Longman.

Lerner, J. (2003) *Learning Disabilities* (9th edn). Boston, MA: Houghton Mifflin.

Mercer, C.D. and Mercer, A.R. (1993) *Teaching Students with Learning Problems* (4th edn). New York: Macmillan.

Rust, J. and Golombok, S. (1999) *Modern Psychometrics: The Science of Psychological Assessment* (2nd edn). London: Routledge.

Wolfendale, S. (ed.) (1993) *Assessing Special Educational Needs.* London: Cassell.

Attentional difficulties

Attention is influenced by a variety of factors, e.g. the novelty, interest, value and difficulty of the task and the pupil's psychological and physical state. In particular pupils need to be willing and able to ignore distractions and interference and concentrate on set tasks. Teaching styles and methods also influence attention. Teachers may not provide sufficiently interesting or engaging tasks, they may fail to present tasks in an interesting format or use inappropriate teaching methods.

Attention can be increased through providing short tasks, breaking long tasks into shorter ones or by providing stimulating and novel tasks. However, attentional difficulties can also be the result of ADD/ADHD, a disorder resulting from what is believed to be a neurotransmitter malfunction in the brain. An attentional difficulty of this kind requires treatment through psychostimulants like Ritalin and/or through behavioural techniques.

Attitudes

Teachers' attitudes towards pupils with learning difficulties may, positively or negatively, affect those pupils and their learning. Such pupils may be perceived negatively as lacking the necessary knowledge, skills and motivation to access the curriculum. Furthermore, they may be seen as unproductive and unrewarding to teach and as a possible source of disruption in the classroom. Teachers may see such pupils as taking up a disproportionate amount of their time at the expense of other pupils. The attitude of pupils with learning difficulties may be positive or negative towards learning. Pupils may see learning as unproductive and irrelevant, a source of anxiety, embarrassment and failure. They may engage in specific behaviours in order to avoid learning, particularly with regard to reading or writing. Specific behaviours might be particular types of off-task behaviour, e.g. arriving late and without equipment, being out of seat, roaming around or leaving the classroom, talking or abusing others, calling out, fidgeting, interfering, making various noises, clowning around or staring into space.

Attribution

Pupils with learning difficulties may attribute their learning problems to internal factors (lack of ability, lack of interest and an inability to concentrate) and they may also attribute their problems to external factors (blaming the teacher or the task). They may also make global attributions that all tasks are difficult or make specific attributions that the set task is too demanding. Stable and unstable factors may also be seen as contributing to learning problems, e.g. that one's ability is fixed and that one's motivation inevitably fluctuates. If learning difficulties are attributed to internal, stable and global factors then pupils are likely to be pessimistic and even fatalistic about their chances of overcoming or ameliorating their learning difficulties.

Fiske, S.T. and Taylor, S.E. (1991) *Social Cognition* (2nd edn). New York: McGraw-Hill.
Forsterling, F. (2001) *Attribution: An Introduction to Theories, Research and Applications*. Hove: Psychology Press.

Attribution retraining

This approach is a strategy or intervention designed to provide pupils with learning difficulties with an internal locus of control. The aim is to encourage those pupils to see their difficulties as not fixed and unchangeable but ones that, with effort and application, can be addressed successfully. Interventions are chosen to demonstrate to pupils that their attributions are incorrect, for example in regarding their lack of ability or the complexity of tasks. Tasks are structured to enable progress in learning to occur and to be maintained. Pupils see that they can achieve success, and by doing so they no longer see themselves as lacking ability or that set tasks are too difficult for them.

Attribution theory

A psychological theory that has its basis in the concept of social cognition. Social cognition is concerned with how people process and interpret information about themselves and others. Attributions are where people attribute or ascribe characteristics, feelings and motives to themselves and others. Attribution theory originates from Heider's theory of the attribution of causality. This theory sees people as attributing causes to either internal personal factors or to external environmental factors or a combination of both.

Attributional style

Pertaining to the tendency for a person to make certain kinds of causal attribution rather than others. Pupils who perceive their difficulties as being due to internal, stable and global factors are said to have a pessimistic attributional style and as a result are likely to avoid challenging tasks or give up easily when obstacles to learning appear.

Forsterling, F. (2001) *Attribution: An Introduction to Theories, Research and Applications*. Hove: Psychology Press.
Heider, F. (1958) *The Psychology of Interpersonal Relations*. New York: Wiley.
Rotter, J.B. (1954) *Social Learning and Clinical Psychology*. Englewood Cliffs, NJ: Prentice-Hall.

Auditory processing

Children who have reading difficulties often display early signs of difficulties with auditory processing. Such children can hear but have problems with phonological awareness, auditory memory, auditory discrimination, auditory sequencing and blending.

Autism

A major type of pervasive developmental disorder (PDD) of early origin which, as a result, affects the whole lifespan. Children with autism show impairments in social interaction and communication, in language development and a lack of pretend or make-believe play. Most children with autism display mental retardation. There can, however, be specific areas of ability. Impairments in social behaviour include lack of social or emotional reciprocity, attachment problems, lack of interest in social relationships, lack of empathy and a lack of sharing of positive feelings with others. There is delayed spoken language development and a variety of pragmatic language (language used for social intentions) peculiarities including echolalia (repeating exactly what has been heard) and neologisms (coining new words or expressions). There is a paucity of social conversation. Behaviour is stereotyped and repetitive and there are persistent demands that routines remain unchanged. There are negative emotional reactions (temper tantrums) in response to attempts to change routines. Feelings are often incongruent with the social context in which they are expressed. As regards the cognitive aspects of autism, about three-quarters of children have IQs below 70. Only about 20 per cent have an IQ within the normal range. Other problems associated with being autistic include fears, phobias, epilepsy, enuresis, encopresis and self-injury such as head banging. Various theories have been suggested for the aetiology or cause of autism including biological and cognitive theories. Biological theories suggest a genetic contribution to autism and a connection to congenital infection and obstetric complications. Cognitive theories suggest that cognitive processing deficits, social understanding deficits and a lack of a 'theory of mind' are contributory factors.

A multi-agency and multi-disciplinary team undertake assessment. Early identification and intervention is essential. The assessment process includes parental and teacher interviews and the psychometric testing of intelligence and language. Interventions include psycho-education, structured educational programmes, behaviour modification, social skills and communication training, and appropriate educational placement. There are various other approaches to the treatment of autism, e.g. Secretin therapy and nutritional therapies to which some parents attest but where there is debate surrounding their efficacy.

Cumin, V., Leach, J. and Stevenson, G. (2000) *Autism in the Early Years*. London: David Fulton Publishers.

Frith, U. (ed.) (1991) *Autism and Asperger Syndrome*. Cambridge: Cambridge University Press.

Howlin, P. (1998) *Children with Autism and Asperger Syndrome: A Guide for Practitioners and Carers*. Chichester: Wiley.

Jordan, R. (1999) *Autistic Spectrum Disorders: An Introductory Handbook for Practitioners*. London: David Fulton Publishers.

Jordan, R. and Jones, G. (1999) *Meeting the Needs of Children with Autistic Spectrum Disorders*. London: David Fulton Publishers.

Jordan, R. *et al.* (1998) *Educational Interventions for Children with Autism: A Literature Review of Recent and Current Research*. Nottingham: DfEE.

Mesibov, G. and Howley, M. (2003) *Accessing the Curriculum for Pupils with Autistic Spectrum Disorders: Using the TEACCH Programme to Help Inclusion*. London. David Fulton Publishers.

Contact

The National Autistic Society, 393 City Road, London EC1 1NG. Tel: 020 7833 2299; Fax: 020 7833 9666; e-mail: nas@nasorg.uk; www.oneworld.org/autism-uk/

Autistic spectrum disorders

The characteristics of autism are wide and varied and can be said to occur along a continuum or spectrum. The severity and variety of autistic characteristics such as social and communication deficits, IQ and language ability may vary between children and within children.

Wing, L. (1996) *The Autistic Spectrum*. London: Constable.

Avoidance behaviour

Children with learning difficulties who have experienced embarrassment, humiliation, anxiety, fear or failure in the learning situation may avoid being in such situations again. As a result children may become absentees or truants. Avoidance behaviour is due in part to classical conditioning where an emotional response becomes paired with, and is later elicited by, a specific stimulus.

Behaviour analysis

A method of analysing learning and behavioural tasks in order to identify the subskills needed to learn a given task or behaviour. These skills are then arranged in a logical and ordered sequence. The students are then taught each subskill in order, to complete the task. This approach can be used to teach reading and other skills.

Alberto, P.A. and Troutman, A.C. (1990) *Applied Behavior Analysis for Teachers* (3rd edn). Columbus, OH: Merrill Publishing Company.

Behaviour management

Where pupils with learning difficulties have behaviour difficulties it will be necessary to resolve those difficulties in order to address learning difficulties. A programme of behaviour management should be implemented. These programmes may be based on different approaches, e.g. behavioural, cognitive-behavioural and person-centred counselling. However, behaviour difficulties may not be simply a function of child deficits (child-deficit model), but may in part result from negative interactions (interactionist model) between children and parents/carers, pupils and pupils, pupils and teachers and pupils and schools.

Emerson, E. (1995) *Challenging Behaviour: Analysis and Intervention in People with Learning Difficulties*. Cambridge: Cambridge University Press.

Behavioural and emotional difficulties

There exists a whole range of emotional and behavioural difficulties that can have a negative effect on learning or can cause learning difficulties. However, it can be difficult to disentangle cause and effect, i.e. whether learning difficulties are the cause or the effect of behaviour difficulties. Emotional difficulties such as anxiety, specific fears, phobias and mood disorders can have a negative impact as can behavioural difficulties such as conduct disorders, oppositional defiant disorders and disruptive behaviour generally. Emotional and behavioural difficulties can interfere with learning processes such as attention, memory, information processing and reasoning. However, learning difficulties can cause emotional and behavioural difficulties through pupils experiencing failure at attempting or performing learning tasks or failing to acquire literacy and numeracy skills.

Ayers, H. and Prytys, C. (2002) *An A to Z Guide to Emotional and Behavioural Difficulties.* London: David Fulton Publishers.

Cooper, P., Smith, C.J. and Upton, G. (1994) *Emotional and Behavioural Difficulties: Theory to Practice.* London: Routledge.

Behavioural teaching methods

Those methods that are based on the application of behavioural psychology to learning difficulties. This approach uses techniques such as an ABC or functional analysis, baseline assessment, target setting, task analysis, modelling, prompting and positive reinforcement. The ABC identifies the antecedents, the consequences and the setting or context that influence learning behaviour. This approach starts off by setting a target skill. A baseline assessment is then undertaken to find out to what extent if any the pupil can perform the target skill. The target skill will need to be broken down into components or steps through task analysis. The pupil is then encouraged to achieve the target skill through a process of positive reinforcement or rewards. Prompting is used to help the pupil to negotiate difficult steps or to remember past steps.

Farrell, P. (1997) *Teaching Pupils with Learning Difficulties.* London: Cassell.

Kazdin, A.E. (1994) *Behavior Modification in Applied Settings* (5th edn). Pacific Grove, CA: Brooks/Cole Publishing.

Behavioural theories of learning

This approach regards all behaviour as learned or as the product of learning and heredity. Learning is strengthened through reinforcement or weakened through punishment. Responses that are reinforced or rewarded are repeated. Those that are punished are reduced or extinguished. Teaching approaches are based on target setting, prompting, cueing, rehearsal, shaping and the positive reinforcement of specific target behaviours. Positive reinforcement is the operant technique most frequently used and recommended; it is preferred to punishment. Positive reinforcers may be material (stickers) or non-material (praise) and are delivered after positive responses, increasing the likelihood of further positive responses. Punishment occurs when an aversive or painful experience is delivered after the performance of a negative response. Punishment may generate a number of undesirable side effects, e.g. anxiety, fear and disaffection with teachers and school, generally. Some operant techniques such as positive reinforcement are used to some extent in direct instruction, especially in structured teaching programmes.

Domjan, M. (1998) *The Principles of Learning and Behavior* (4th edn). Pacific Grove, CA: Brooks/Cole Publishing.

Lieberman, D.A. (1993) *Learning: Behavior and Cognition* (2nd edn). Pacific Grove, CA: Brooks/Cole Publishing Company

Benchmarks and benchmarking

Benchmarks are short-term objectives that are employed to move pupils from their current performance levels to their long-term objectives. A number of benchmarks are used and they are usually sequential and specific in terms of learning tasks and criteria. The benchmarks should be manageable for pupils and their teachers. Benchmarking is a method of comparing performance levels of a group so that similar individuals can compare their performance levels with that of others in the group. The benchmark set will be the performance level achieved by those who are the more successful members of the group.

Birth problems

There are various problems before (prenatal), during (perinatal) and after birth (postnatal) that can contribute to learning difficulties. Prenatal problems include infections (cytomegalovirus CMV infection), substance abuse such as abuse of alcohol (foetal alcohol syndrome), malnutrition and dietary deficiencies and imbalances. Perinatal problems include asphyxia (suffocation resulting in anoxia). Postnatal problems include infections, malnutrition, toxins and accidental and non-accidental cerebral trauma.

Brain damage

There are various disorders of the central nervous system that affect learning and cognitive functions as well as affecting other functions. For example, seizure disorders can be associated with learning disabilities. Traumatic brain injury is an acquired disability due to accidents or inflicted injuries.

Banich, M.T. (1997) *Neuropsychology: The Neural Bases of Mental Function*. Boston, MA: Houghton Mifflin.

Tyler, J.S. and Mira, M.P. (1999) *Traumatic Brain Injury in Children and Adolescents: A Sourcebook for Teachers and other School Personnel* (2nd edn). Austin, TX: ProEd.

Brain-injured children

Traumatic brain injuries are very common in children. They are acquired injuries caused by an external force that results in total or partial functional disability and/or psychosocial difficulties. Injuries can range from mild to severe and it is difficult to predict recovery. The areas affected by brain injury can include cognition, memory, attention, thinking and reasoning, sensory, perceptual and motor abilities. The term is not applied to those children who are born with brain damage. Types of injury include motor vehicle and cycle accidents, falls, sporting injuries and child abuse. The effects of brain damage are likely to exacerbate any pre-existing disabilities. The signs of brain injury include perceptual and motor problems, headaches, tiredness, spasticity (sudden muscle contractions and tightening), seizures and paralysis. There may also be social, behavioural or emotional problems such as sudden mood changes, anxiety, depression, relationship difficulties, hyperactivity and also motivational problems. Children may experience difficulties with short- and long-term memory, with concentration and with reading, writing and planning.

Walker, S. and Wicks, B. (2003) *Educating Children with Acquired Brain Injury*. London: David Fulton Publishers.

Broca's aphasia

This type of aphasia is characterised by impairment of auditory language comprehension, speech errors and neologisms.

Calculator use

The use of a calculator is considered to be helpful in teaching arithmetical operations (particularly multiplication and division) to pupils who have learning difficulties. This is particularly the case in the areas of recall and retention that are required for computations. Pupils with learning difficulties who have persistent problems with these aspects can benefit from using a calculator. Calculator use also assists in the development of automaticity. The use of a calculator enables pupils to put their efforts into understanding mathematical concepts and problem solving rather than just performing computations.

Children with learning difficulties

Learning difficulties have been defined through norm-referenced IQ testing and through the use of norm-referenced developmental scales. They have also been defined in terms of different types of curricular need and the age at which learning problems first appear. A definitive definition is not considered possible. In practice, those pupils who have learning difficulties are seen as lying along a continuum from mild through moderate to severe. The prevalence rate has been stated as somewhere between 12 and 30 per cent of the school population. These children tend to have lower achievement levels and are slower in negotiating developmental stages or coping with developmental tasks. Many of those with mild to moderate difficulties only become noticeable when they enter primary or even secondary education. They are often poor in their use of expressive language, showing poor comprehension and manifesting slow progress in acquiring literacy and numeracy skills. Additionally, they may lack strategies for organising and using appropriate knowledge and skills. Their social skills may also be inadequate and they may have emotional and behavioural difficulties. Teachers tend to attribute learning difficulties to within child factors and emotional and behavioural difficulties to home circumstances and/or parents or carers. These children may also have attentional, auditory and visual difficulties. Children with a variety or range of difficulties are described as having complex learning difficulties. Children with mild or moderate difficulties frequently display the following characteristics: a low level of retention, a restricted vocabulary, monosyllabic responses to questioning, limited oral and written expression, difficulties in generalisation and problems in transferring knowledge and skills from one context to another.

Farrell, P. (1997) *Teaching Pupils with Learning Difficulties: Strategies and Solutions*. London: Cassell.

Leach, D.J. and Raybould, E.C. (1977) *Learning and Behaviour Difficulties in School*. London: Open Books.

Learner, J. (2003) *Learning Disabilities* (9th edn). Boston, MA:. Houghton Mifflin.

Mercer, C.D. and Mercer, A.R. (1993) *Teaching Students with Learning Problems* (4th edn). New York: Merrill.

Montgomery, D. (1990) *Children with Learning Difficulties*. London: Cassell.

Westwood, P. (2004) *Learning and Learning Difficulties: A Handbook for Teachers*. London: David Fulton Publishers.

Children at risk

Children at risk of developing learning difficulties include those who experience a range of environmental risks. These include parental substance abuse, parental child abuse and neglect, parental learning disabilities, low level of parental education, negative parental attitudes to education, family disorganisation, family social isolation and social and economic deprivation. Prenatal substance abuse is also a risk factor.

Children with Specific Learning Difficulties (SpLD)

Children with SpLD are usually defined through negation. In other words those pupils who have at least average intelligence whose learning difficulties are not explained through visual or hearing difficulties, health problems, emotional and behavioural difficulties or socio-economic disadvantage. However, pupils with SpLD may experience emotional and behavioural difficulties due to their specific learning difficulties. They are also assumed to have experienced effective teaching. However, it should be noted that these pupils do not form a homogeneous group, some pupils possessing skills that others lack. Even though there is an absence of negative factors, these pupils have not acquired basic skills in literacy and numeracy. There may also exist inadequate skills in the areas of receptive and expressive oral language and social development. These pupils are identified as manifesting a discrepancy between measured IQ (WISC IV tests) and achievement. There is considerable and unexpected underachievement that cannot be explained through low intelligence or low ability. These pupils are differentiated from other pupils whose learning difficulties are due to negative factors such as low IQ or inadequate teaching. Pupils with SpLD may have emotional and behavioural difficulties but these are seen as effects of SpLD, not causes. There are various types of SpLD, such as reading disability (dyslexia), arithmetical and mathematical disabilities (dyscalculia), writing disabilities (dysgraphia) and spelling and recall difficulties. Any pupil may have difficulties in one or more areas. There are various estimates of the prevalence of SpLD, from 1 to 30 per cent of the school population. As with many estimates of the prevalence of psychological characteristics, conditions or disorders, they often vary according to the criteria used for identification. It may also be claimed that over- or under-identification have occurred due to different criteria being applied or as a result of criteria not being applied correctly. Another problem arises in terms of the cut-off points for what is regarded as normal intelligence. Different cut-off points will also affect estimates of prevalence. Identification and assessment of pupils with SpLD has been by using a discrepancy for-mula based on tested IQ and achievement levels. Another type of assessment is through assessing SpLD pupils' responses to various kinds of intervention. Various causes have been suggested for SpLD including genetic and neurological factors. Other causes suggested include inadequate phonological processing and weaknesses in automatised lexical retrieving. Visual perceptual difficulties are not seen as affecting many pupils with SpLD. Various interventions have been suggested for addressing SpLD including teaching to improve recall, teaching comprehension strategies, direct instruction, behavioural and precision teaching. A carefully structured curriculum is also recommended.

Lerner, J. (2003) *Learning Disabilities* (9th edn). Boston, MA: Houghton Mifflin.
Westwood, P. (2004) *Learning and Learning Difficulties*. London: David Fulton Publishers.

Chromosomal abnormalities

These are defects or errors in genetic transmission that occur at the chromosomal level. Chromosomes are structures within cells that contain thousands of gene pairs that determine physical traits and direct the growth of physical and biochemical systems. Chromosomal abnormalities generally result from random errors that occur when an egg or sperm cell is developing. During cell division an error may occur that results in an egg or sperm cell having too many or too few chromosomes. Many, but not all, children with chromosomal abnormalities experience learning difficulties. A common example is trisomy 21, referred to as Down's syndrome (most frequent error is on the 21st chromosome which has an extra chromosome). Down's syndrome can also result from unbalanced translocation where a part of a chromosome becomes joined to another chromosome or becomes a part of another chromosome. Chromosomal abnormalities of sex-linked chromosomes are correlated with a higher-than-average incidence of speech, reading and learning difficulties. Some rare disorders are the result of small chromosomal changes, for example Prader-Willi syndrome (extreme obesity, learning difficulties) is caused by a minute deletion on chromosome 15.

Class size

The effect of class size on pupil learning and behaviour is an ongoing debate. There is not necessarily a direct relationship between small class size and improved learning outcomes. Teaching style and methods also impact on learning and behaviour. Reducing class size does not, by itself, improve learning. Inappropriate teaching methods may offset the effects of reduced class size. However, there are benefits in reducing class size to less than twenty pupils, having smaller classes in the early years, having smaller classes for those pupils who come from socially and economically deprived backgrounds and for those pupils at risk. Children with learning difficulties can also benefit from small classes or groups.

Classroom environment

Certain types of environmental factors can adversely affect pupil's learning performances and, in particular, pupils with learning difficulties. These factors include high noise levels, multiple sources of distraction, high or low temperatures, inadequate ventilation, crowded or cluttered space and particular group seating arrangements.

Clinical teaching

An approach to helping children with learning difficulties that does not depend on any particular type of instruction, setting or teaching style. The aim of this approach is to match teaching and learning opportunities to pupils' specific learning needs. Clinical teaching focuses on strengths as well as weaknesses. The assessment process concentrates on what pupils are capable of as well as the types of errors they make in learning. It adopts a test–teach–test procedure with teachers combining the functions of testing and teaching. The stages of this cyclical approach are assessment, planning, implementation, evaluation and, if necessary, reassessment and the introduction of new forms of the stages in a continuous cycle of teaching.

Lerner, J. (2003) *Learning Disabilities* (9th edn). Boston, MA: Houghton Mifflin.

Cloze procedure

A technique for developing language and comprehension skills. It is a Gestalt type procedure that requires pupils to place appropriate words in gaps in text where particular lexical (nouns, verbs, adverbs, adjectives) and/or structural words (conjunctions, prepositions) have been deleted. It is both a form of testing and a way of teaching reading comprehension and language skills.

Code of Practice (COP) (Revised 2001)

In England a revised Code of Practice (DfES 2001) has come into being which includes statutory duties that are defined by the Special Needs and Disability Act 2001. The IEP (Individual Action Plan) is an essential element of the COP and states how support is to be provided. Where a pupil is assessed as needing support an IEP is drawn up by the SENCO in liaison with the class and subject teachers and the pupil and parents/carers. If at the IEP review the pupil is still not making sufficient or any progress through School Action, then School Action Plus is initiated whereby the SENCO organises a review meeting with parents/carers and external specialists or professionals. A new IEP is drawn up with the advice and support of the external professionals and regularly reviewed. If School Action Plus fails to meet the needs of the pupil then the SENCO may suggest that the pupil be considered for statutory assessment.

Drifte, C. (2003) *Handbook for Pre-School SEN Provision: The Code of Practice in Relation to the Early Years* (2nd edn). London: David Fulton Publishers.

Goddard, C. and Tester, G. (1996) *SEN Legislation and the Code of Practice: A Whole School Approach*. London: David Fulton Publishers.

Ramjhun, A. (2002) *Implementing the Code of Practice for Children with Special Educational Needs* (2nd edn). London: David Fulton Publishers.

Cognitive abilities

These include thinking, reasoning, planning and conceptual developmental abilities. These abilities are generally seen as being the result of both heredity and the environment, but there is controversy regarding the extent to which these factors influence cognitive ability.

Cognitive strategies

These are teaching strategies based on cognitive approaches to learning. They include helping pupils to construct their own knowledge, building on pupils' existing knowledge and skills, determining the correct level of difficulty for pupils (zone of proximal development), providing the right level of support for pupils (scaffolding), facilitating automaticity in knowledge and skills and motivating pupils.

Dockrell, J. and McShane, J. (1992) *Children's Learning Difficulties: A Cognitive Approach*. Oxford: Blackwell.

Cognitive-behavioural theories of learning

Types of cognitive and behavioural approaches that combine elements of both approaches. Changes in learning are seen as resulting from interactions between the environment and the cognitive processes of the learner. Cognitive processes such as thinking and reasoning mediate environmental factors or influences. Approaches based on this theory of learning use teaching methods such as graphic organisers (visual representation of concepts) as, for example, in Venn diagrams, word webs, concept maps and mind mapping. Another important element of this theory of learning is metacognition. Metacognition refers to a learner's knowledge and their understanding of the cognitive processes underlying their own thinking and reasoning. Metacognitive strategies are those methods that encourage pupils to think or reflect on their own learning processes as a way of improving or enhancing their learning.

Eysenck, M.W. (ed.) (1994) *The Blackwell Dictionary of Cognitive Psychology*. Oxford: Blackwell Publishers.

Eysenck, M.W. and Keane, M.T. (1995) *Cognitive Psychology: A Student's Handbook* (3rd edn). Hove: Lawrence Erlbaum Associates.

Sheldon, B. (1995) *Cognitive-Behavioural Therapy: Research, Practice and Philosophy.* London: Routledge.

Westwood. P. (2004) *Learning and Learning Difficulties.* London: David Fulton Publishers.

Collaborative learning

This approach aims to encourage individual pupils or groups of pupils to collaborate or co-operate with other pupils in order to attempt and complete learning tasks.

Communication skills

Speech and language difficulties are common precursors of learning difficulties. Children with communication difficulties have difficulties listening and understanding others, in responding appropriately to others and in initiating and engaging in communication with others.

Comprehension

Poor comprehension of text may be due to poor text-processing strategies, poor motivation, lack of interest or relevance of the text, inadequate general word or specialist subject vocabulary, poor word identification and a lack of strategies for identifying ideas and detail in the text.

Computational skills

Basic computational skills are necessary for problem solving in mathematics. Learners should be able to add, subtract, multiply and divide. Pupils with SpLD experience many problems in the area of computation. Teachers can devise computational tests or they can access published tests in order to assess proficiency levels in computation. A pupil's problems should be assessed in terms of underlying deficits such as visual, perceptual, spatial and memory deficits. Pupils need to memorise computational facts. This can be achieved through providing pupils with a variety of learning opportunities such as playing games, taking speed tests or using flash cards. The use of concrete and manipulative materials and objects helps move pupils to more abstract and symbolic levels.

Computer-assisted learning

Children with learning difficulties can benefit from the many functions provided by computers. The computer can give children a sense of empowerment and control. Computers can help children to become independent, to develop self-help skills, to develop their cognitive, language and motor skills and also to develop visual and auditory concepts. The use of word processors has enabled children with learning difficulties to create and edit texts and has encouraged and motivated them to write. Computers also provide immediate corrective feedback on spelling and grammar. There are also benefits from using other computer functions such as writing and sending e-mails and searching the internet for information. Computers can also be used for teaching oral language skills. Computer software programs are available to support reading, writing and mathematics and are found in software catalogues.

Cooper, J.D. (2000) *Literacy: Helping Children Construct Meaning* (4th edn). Boston: Houghton Mifflin.
Ott, P. (1997) *How to Detect and Manage Dyslexia*. Oxford: Heinemann.

Confidence

Pupils with learning difficulties often lack self-confidence and fear failure. As a consequence they may not make the effort to learn or may easily give up even when they have acquired the knowledge and skills to succeed.

Constructivist theory of learning

The constructivist approach regards learning as being constructed through the cognitive processes and experiences of particular learners. It is based on the principles of L.S. Vygotsky and J. S. Bruner. This approach is pupil-centred and is based on collaborative group work and problem-solving activities. Pupils engage in exploratory activities and tasks set by teachers. Teachers are required to facilitate the exploratory and discovery activities of their pupils. How far this approach can be effective with pupils with learning difficulties is a moot point.

Bruner, J.S. (1966) *Towards a Theory of Instruction*. Cambridge, MA: Harvard University Press.
Vygotsky, L.S. (1962) *Thought and Language*. Cambridge, MA: MIT Press.

Contextual cues

Contextual cues help pupils to recognise a word through the meaning or context of a sentence or paragraph in which it is embedded. Pupils with learning difficulties, when reading stories, learn to use contextual cues in understanding unfamiliar words.

Co-teaching

This type of teaching occurs when two teachers in the classroom are paired together and, in effect, share the teaching. This pairing usually takes the form of a subject or class teacher paired with a specialist teacher. In the classroom, co-teaching can take a variety of forms such as one teacher being the main or primary teacher, the other having a supporting role. Co-teaching can also take the form of parallel teaching, alternative teaching and team teaching.

Counting skills

A necessary basis for developing numeracy. Many children acquire counting skills incidentally. However, some children who have restricted preschool experiences or are developmentally delayed may not develop a concept of number and may not have any number recognition skills. In these cases children need to be directly taught number facts and number recognition. There are various counting strategies for moving beyond the simple counting of a small group of elements. These strategies can commence with two small groups of a given size. One is the 'count-all' strategy (that is counting all the elements of the groups beginning with one). Another strategy is the 'min' strategy (starting with the larger number and counting on smaller number). The memorising of number facts is necessary if simple mental addition and subtraction are to be performed.

Bley, N.S. and Thornton, C.A. (1995) *Teaching Mathematics to Students with Learning Difficulties.* (3rd edn). Austin, TX: ProEd.

Criterion-referenced tests

These tests measure a pupil's specific knowledge or skills. A particular criterion is established and after pupils meet that criterion or performance level they are taught the knowledge or skills to meet the next criterion. Criterion tests describe rather than compare performances, unlike norm-referenced tests where pupils are directly compared to one another. By using criterion-referenced tests it can be established that pupils have mastered or acquired knowledge or skills.

Curriculum

Curriculum content can be a contributory factor to learning difficulties. The content may be introduced at a too-difficult level and the introduction of new content may be too fast. Pupils with learning difficulties, particularly at secondary level, may not be able to cope with the demands of subject content and may find the pace of instruction and delivery too rapid. They may find it difficult to make connections between their prior learning and current learning. This may lead to fragmented or partial learning or even unlearning. In turn this may result in low self-esteem and motivational problems. For pupils with learning difficulties the curriculum content, according to Brennan, should observe the 4Rs – the content should be real, relevant, realistic and rational. 'Real' meaning that the content relates to their experience, 'relevant' that the content is useful to them, 'realistic' that the content can be learned by them, and 'rational' that the content has value for them.

Brennan, W. (1985) *Curriculum for Special Needs.* Milton Keynes: Open University Press.

Curriculum-based assessment

This type of assessment assesses a pupil in terms of the curricular demands or course content of the curriculum in the pupil's own school or classroom. Targets are set and the pupil's progress towards those targets is measured and recorded. Progress can be illustrated or graphed so that it is observable to both the pupil and the teacher. It enables teachers to observe the progress a pupil makes over time. This form of assessment can be used to monitor progress in reading.

Jones, C.J. (1998) *Curriculum-based Assessment the Easy Way.* Springfield, IL: Charles C. Thomas Publishers.

Shapiro, E.S. (1989) *Academic Skills Problems: Direct Assessment and Intervention.* New York: Guilford Press.

Shinn, M.R. (1989) *Curriculum-based Measurement: Assessing Special Children.* New York: Guilford Press.

D

Deaf pupils

Hearing impairment can have a significant bearing on learning. In addition, many pupils can experience temporary hearing loss through infected tonsils and wax in the ears. The common ear condition otitis media, the inflammation of the middle ear, can also adversely affect learning. The cause of this condition can be infections, allergies or inflamed tonsils or adenoids. This condition can interfere with language development and with auditory perception and can also cause learning difficulties. Pupils with impaired learning often have difficulties with grammar, syntax, vocabulary, comprehension and communication. Their acquisition of reading, spelling and writing skills is often delayed. Their lack of metacognitive knowledge also affects the development of self-regulatory and problem-solving skills.

Watson, L. Gregory, S. and Powers, S. (1999) *Deaf and Hearing Impaired Pupils in Mainstream Schools*. London: David Fulton Publishers.

Decoding

The process of segmenting or breaking down words into their component sounds.

Deficit model

This model sees learning difficulties as being mainly due to deficits or internal factors within the pupil rather than to external factors. Learning difficulties from this perspective are caused by factors such as sensory impairment, low ability, medical conditions, emotional and behavioural problems and specific information processing problems. External factors are seen as less important or as insignificant. External factors include poor teaching, inappropriate curriculum and poor school attendance. An interactionist model or perspective sees learning difficulties as being due to an interaction between both internal and external factors.

Depression

Pupils with learning difficulties can feel depressed for a number of reasons: they can become depressed when they experience failure in learning; they may become depressed if they engage in negative self-evaluation through comparing their performance with peers; or they can experience depression if they suffer peer rejection.

Goodyer, I.M. (ed.) (2001) *The Depressed Child and Adolescent* (2nd edn). Cambridge: Cambridge University Press.

Developmental delay

A term that characterises a pupil as being delayed or behind with respect to a specific developmental stage or phase such as in cognitive, emotional, behavioural, communication, motor or sensory development.

Developmental psychology

This approach identifies and explains psychological development as occurring through maturation, that is by passing through sequence of stages or phases, e.g. Piaget's stages of development. These stages are linked with different ages or developmental milestones. A pupil's capacity for future learning is seen as being dependent on the particular stage the pupil has reached. Pupils are seen as maturing at different rates and the same pupils can be seen as experiencing different rates of development in their abilities. These maturational lags may disappear later on in adolescence or in adulthood as a result of late or delayed maturation. This approach can also see some curriculum demands as presenting learning tasks for pupils before they are ready to cope. Thus the curriculum can be seen as a contributory factor in exacerbating a pupil's learning difficulties. Vygotsky suggested that teaching should be directed towards a pupil's zone of proximal development where tasks are presented that are challenging and that are able to build on the pupil's existing levels of knowledge and skills. Pupils with learning difficulties often need extra time and support to experience success. In particular, pupils with reading difficulties often display maturational delays including that of phonological awareness.

Piaget, J. (1929) *The Child's Conception of the World*. New York: Harcourt Brace.

Slater, A. and Muir, D. (eds) (1999) *The Blackwell Reader in Developmental Psychology*. Oxford: Blackwell.

Smith, P.K., Cowie, H. and Blades, M. (1998) *Understanding Children's Development* (3rd edn). Oxford: Blackwell.

Talay-Ongan, A. (1998) *Typical and Atypical Development in Early Childhood: The Fundamentals:* Leicester: BPS Books.

Vygotsky, L.S. (1962) *Thought and Language*. Cambridge, MA: MIT Press.

Diagnostic assessment

Diagnostic assessment is assessment through testing. Testing is used to identify the specific nature and, if possible, the cause(s) of a difficulty, disability, disorder or syndrome. Many diagnostic tests test general cognitive abilities and also specific skills such as reading, writing, spelling, language and motor skills. Diagnostic manuals such as DSM IV (APA 1994) and ICD-10 (WHO 1992, 1996) are used to diagnose psychiatric and psychological disorders.

Diagnostic tests

Diagnostic tests usually relate to a norm or criterion and provide information about a pupil's strengths and weaknesses. These tests include tests for cognitive abilities, for reading skills, tests for evaluating motor performance, tests for language skills and for identifying sensory deficits. Some types of tests, e.g. intelligence tests are required to be administered by educational psychologists. Intelligence tests are administered to pupils with learning difficulties, e.g. WISC-III (Weschler Intelligence Scale for Children, Third Edition). There is now a revised edition, WISC-IV. The WISC-III provides three IQ scores: Verbal IQ, Performance IQ and Full-scale IQ. It comprises 13 subtests divided into two groups – verbal and performance. With regard to specific learning disability (SpLD), intelligence tests have been used to identify a discrepancy between a pupil's potential ability as measured by an IQ test and levels of achievement attained in subject areas. Intelligence tests have also been used to diagnose a pupil's cognitive strengths and weaknesses and to design and deliver interventions based on that diagnosis.

Diagnostic-prescriptive teaching

This type of teaching takes place when teachers continue to collect assessment information when teaching pupils. The teacher, when testing the pupil, learns what the pupil can or cannot do and, in the light of that, reviews teaching methods and materials. Teaching methods and materials are matched to the pupil's preferences and strengths, e.g. phonics for pupils with auditory strengths and 'whole-word recognition' for pupils with visual strengths. However, since reading requires the integration of both auditory and visual skills, teaching methods need to include both auditory and visual components.

Collins, M. and Cheek, E.H. (1984) *Diagnostic-Prescriptive Reading Instruction: A Guide for Classroom Teachers* (2nd edn). Dubuque, IA: Brown.

Differentiation

Differentiation refers to the adaptation or modification of the content of the delivered curriculum and of teaching and learning strategies to address the needs of specific pupils or groups of pupils. Differentiation may be required so that pupils with learning difficulties can access the curriculum. The curriculum may need to be differentiated or modified to meet or match their needs and abilities. The delivery of instruction and instructional material may also need to be differentiated.

O'Brien, T. and Guiney, D. (2001) *Differentiation in Teaching and Learning: Principles and Practice*. London: Continuum.

Difficulty level

Difficulty level refers to the difficulty of tasks, texts and other teaching materials. Pupils can be failing because tasks and materials are too difficult and the required level of performance is beyond their existing capacities or ability. It is important for teachers to choose the correct level of difficulty for a lesson. Vygotsky's theory of the zone of proximal development is useful in ensuring that teachers present tasks that are neither too easy nor too difficult but are at a midpoint where the tasks are challenging but not beyond their pupils' capabilities.

Direct instruction

This approach has its basis in behavioural teaching. Direct instruction or explicit teaching emphasises the importance of teachers being clear as to the specific skills to be taught and to teach explicitly each step or skill in a structured classroom environment. The teacher controls and directs learning in a sequenced and structured approach using materials that are also sequenced and structured. Targets must be specific and clear to pupils and the teacher should monitor progress in relation to those targets providing immediate feedback to pupils. Direct instruction is used particularly in the teaching of basic skills.

Wilen, W., Ishler, M., Hutchinson, J. and Kindsvatter, R. (2000) *Dynamics of Effective Teaching* (4th edn). New York: Wiley.

Directed reading activity

A method of teaching reading comprehension by requiring learners to read a passage of text, then requesting them to predict what will happen and asking them to check whether they are correct or not in their predictions.

Discrepancy formulae

Mathematical methods and calculations or formulae used in ability-achievement discrepancy analysis to measure the discrepancy between a pupil's potential and his/her actual achievement. IQ-achievement discrepancy has been used as the primary criterion for identifying SpLD.

Rust, J. and Golumbok, S. (1999) *Modern Psychometrics: The Science of Psychological Assessment.* London: Routledge.

Distractibility

This term refers to a pupil's lack of ability in concentrating on learning tasks or attending to a teacher's instructions. Pupils with learning difficulties are frequently distractible.

Down's syndrome or Down syndrome

Down's syndrome is a medical condition that has its basis in a chromosomal aberration (three copies of chromosome 21 or trisomy 21). In a small number of cases chromosomal structure is affected due to the processes of translocation and mosaicism. In these cases intellectual disability and physical differences may not be so marked. The incidence of Down's syndrome is approximately one in 700 live births but increases with maternal age, particularly after the age of 35. Down's syndrome is a common cause of intellectual disability. Most children with the syndrome have a mild to moderate intellectual disability although small numbers have a severe form and others are in the low normal to normal intelligence range. Physical symptoms include: oblique eyes; low muscle tone (hypotonia); small, low-set ears; short stature; fine skin and hair; and heart, digestive and skeletal malformations. There are various medical complications that can be associated with the condition including congenital heart defects, upper respiratory infections, gastrointestinal blockage symptoms, visual defects (strabismus, nystagmus and cataracts), hearing difficulties (middle ear infections and conductive hearing loss), dental problems, obesity, hypothyroidism, depression and joint dislocations. Many of these medical complications are treatable. Longevity is usually from 40 to 50 years but has increased due to medical intervention. In later life there is a risk of developing Alzheimer's disease. Significant cognitive and language delays become observable by the first birthday. There can be significant memory problems in recall and recognition along with semantic delay or deficiency due to a symbolic processing deficit. Children with Down's syndrome may also have a deficit when it comes to learning, using and understanding grammatical expressions. Pupils with Down's syndrome may use one-word utterances to convey complex ideas. Phonological errors are usually apparent in the form of fricative phonemes such as f, v, s, z, sh and th. There can also be pragmatic deficits in the form of not maintaining interpersonal distance and not adequately attending to or responding to non-verbal communication. Children with Down's syndrome have been successfully included in mainstream schools and classrooms.

Lorenz, S. (1998) *Children with Down's Syndrome: A Guide for Teachers and Learning Support Assistants in Mainstream Primary and Secondary Schools.* London: David Fulton Publishers.

Contact

Down's Syndrome Association, Langdon Down Centre, 2a Langdon Park, London TW11 9PS. Tel: 0845 230 0372; Fax: 0845 230 0373; e-mail: info@downs-syndrome.org.uk; www.downs-syndrome.org.uk

Dynamic assessment

This is an interactive and an additional form of assessment that focuses on the ability of a learner to respond to different types of intervention. It is based on the principle that all pupils are capable of changing or modifying their learning processes. Teachers intervene during the assessment process itself in order to bring about changes in the pupil's development. This assessment also focuses on the pupil's problem-solving abilities and any factors that encourage, prevent or hinder the pupil's learning. The pupil's responses and reactions to interventions are seen as providing essential information concerning the effectiveness of those interventions. The type of assessment is usually administered through the form of a pretest–intervention–retest process. There are various dynamic assessment procedures including open-ended and standardised interventions involving problem-solving tasks, a graduated prompting and hinting process for incorrect responses and curriculum-based interventions that encompass good practice.

Dyscalculia

Developmental dyscalculia is a specific learning disability in mathematics and does not refer to low achievement in mathematics generally. It is thought to have a genetic and neurological basis and is a disability that prevents the acquisition of mathematical skills in an otherwise normal child. In the DSM IV (APA 1994), the term 'mathematics disorder' is used and it is described as a disorder where mathematical ability is below what would be expected from the learner's age, intelligence and education. The ICD-10 (WHO 1992, 1996) uses the term specific disorder of arithmetic skills. Pupils with dyscalculia find difficulty in recalling number facts and in learning mathematical terms and symbols. They also find it difficult to calculate, to use algorithms, to reason mathematically and to use appropriate mathematical strategies. These difficulties are found in other pupils but in comparison with a control group their problems are more severe. Underlying deficits in pupils with dyscalculia include deficits in spatial organisation (reversals and transpositions of numbers) and graphic skills (untidy presentation of mathematical work). There is also inattention to detail (omitting numbers, signs and decimal points), inflexibility (unable to change operations), ineffective procedural processes (inaccurate algorithms) and memory deficits (poor recall of number facts). Suggested causes for dyscalculia include auditory and visual perceptual processing difficulties and inadequate use of, or lack of capacity in, working memory.

Dysgraphia

This term refers to extremely poor or very inadequate handwriting skills. It may represent underlying deficits such as fine-motor difficulties or an inability to perform the fine-motor movements required to write or copy letters or words. There may also be poor visual perception of letters and words and difficulties in visual memory. Strategies for improving handwriting skills include: writing movement practice through using finger painting or writing in a sand tray, ensuring a comfortable writing position, orientating the paper correctly, ensuring the correct pencil or pen grip, using stencils and templates for practising letter and number formation and tracing letters. Teaching keyboard or typing skills are also useful for pupils who have poor handwriting skills. Recently, the term has come to encompass other aspects of writing such as written expression, clarity and spelling.

Dyslexia

There are different definitions and identification criteria for dyslexia and, as a result, there has been some controversy over the nature of dyslexia and its prevalence. There are concerns regarding possible over- or under-identification of dyslexia. Dyslexia is now generally accepted as a reading disability and is categorised as a severe, persistent reading difficulty that is not the result of low cognitive ability. Writing, spelling and speaking difficulties may also be associated with dyslexia. Dyslexia is not due to sensory impairment, poor learning opportunities or inadequate teaching. Dyslexia is the most common type of specific learning disability (SpLD); others include dyscalculia and dyspraxia. Various dyslexia subtypes have been described. A number of factors are believed to be associated with dyslexia including heredity (family studies and twin studies), neurological ('soft' signs, subtle and minor symptoms and anomalies in brain structure and function), poor phonological awareness (inability to decompose words into sounds and to recall sounds from memory), weakness in rapid automatic naming (problems in rapid naming of letters and numbers), visual perception (weakness in visual skills), and poor learning style (poor concentration, distractibility, impulsivity and poor self-correction).

Dyslexia includes difficulties in working memory, difficulties with automaticity, especially in the areas of literacy and numeracy, problems with phonological processing and visual perceptual difficulties. Although dyslexic pupils have difficulties they can also have certain strengths such as in the areas of problem solving and analytic and creative thinking. Dyslexia spans social class and ability range. It is more common among boys but may be under-diagnosed among girls, and can persist into adulthood. Indicators depending on age include reading, spelling, writing and number difficulties. With regard to reading problems these include poor rhyme and alliteration identification, a high number of reading errors, failure to recognise high-frequency words, word reversal, and the avoidance of reading. With respect to spelling, it is below chronological age, it is phonetic but incorrect, syllables and parts of a sound blend are omitted, and there is letter reversal and poor letter formation. Writing is characterised by poor letter formation, words and endings left out, little or no punctuation, number, letter or word reversal, messy work and difficulty in copying or with dictation. With regard to number, there will often be difficulties in learning tables, number facts, mental arithmetic and reversing single or double digits.

There may be other difficulties that accompany dyslexia including ADHD, dyspraxia, poor motor co-ordination, handwriting difficulties, inadequate organisational skills and a poor memory. Pupils with dyslexia may also experience low self-esteem and become withdrawn, anxious or disruptive. These pupils may be fearful and anxious about tasks requiring literacy and numeracy skills. Motivation and attention may suffer. It has been suggested that dyslexia is a neurological disorder that takes the form of structural and functional differences in the brain of dyslexics. It is also thought to have a genetic component. Identification and assessment of dyslexia has usually been through intelligence testing. There are also other assessment instruments including baseline assessment, checklists, diagnostic measures and curriculum-based assessment. The aim of intelligence testing is to identify a discrepancy between a pupil's measured IQ and his/her achievement or attainment in subject areas. Different types of discrepancy formulae have been used to measure the gap between measured ability and achievement. Criticisms have been made of the use of such formulae along the lines that they are incompatible with early intervention, that they do not necessarily predict learning potential, including progress in reading, and that they do not necessarily predict which pupils will benefit from which interventions. It has been suggested that response to different levels of intervention is a more effective method of assessing such pupils.

Various types of intervention have been implemented including teaching pupils how to learn, teaching to improve recall, teaching reading comprehension strategies, direct instruction, precision teaching, computer-aided instruction, visual-perceptual and perceptual-motor training, social skills training and dietary regimes. Effective interventions are said to be those that encourage pupils to acquire and to implement learning strategies, e.g. phonemic decoding strategies. Behavioural and direct teaching methods are also said to be effective in the instruction of pupils. For the early years, specific interventions include phonological activities, syllable identification, blending and deletion, rhyme awareness, phoneme blending and deletion, developing listening skills and improving fine motor skills. During the middle and secondary years, effective approaches include precision and multi-sensory teaching. Furthermore, IEPs should be drawn up specifying SMART targets, success criteria, teaching methods and resources.

British Dyslexia Association (2002) *BDA Handbook*. Reading: BDA.

Henderson, A. (1998) *Maths for the Dyslexic: A Practical Guide*. London: David Fulton Publishers.

Kay, J. and Yeo, D. (2003) *Dyslexia and Maths*. London: David Fulton Publishers.

Keates, A. (2002) *Dyslexia and ICT: A Guide for Teachers and Parents* (2nd edn). London: David Fulton Publishers.

Lerner, J. W. (2003) *Learning Disabilities* (9th edn). Boston, MA: Houghton Mifflin.

Peer, L. and Reid, G. (eds) (2001) *Dyslexia – Successful Inclusion in the Secondary School*. London: David Fulton Publishers.

Peer, L. and Reid, G. (2003) *Introduction to Dyslexia*. London: David Fulton Publishers.

Riddick, B., Wolfe, J. and Lumsdon, D. (2002) *Dyslexia: A Practical Guide for Teachers and Parents*. London: David Fulton Publishers.

Walton. M. (1998) *Teaching Reading and Spelling to Dyslexic Children*. London: David Fulton Publishers.

Westwood, P. (2004) *Learning and Learning Difficulties*. London: David Fulton Publishers.

Contacts

British Dyslexia Association, 98 London Road, Reading RG1 5AU. Tel: 0118 966 8271; Fax: 0118 935 1927; e-mail: helpline@bdadyslexia.org.uk; www.bda-dyslexia.org.uk
Dyslexia Institute, Wick Road, Egham, Surrey TW20 OHH, Tel: 01784 222300; Fax: 01784 222300; e-mail: info@dyslexia-inst.org.uk; www.dyslexia-inst.org.uk

Dyspraxia or developmental dyspraxia

Developmental dyspraxia is an impairment or severe difficulty in the planning and organisation of physical movement. It is defined in the COP as a specific learning difficulty. It is believed to be four times more common among boys than girls and sometimes runs in families. Symptoms occur at an early age in the form of failure to meet certain developmental milestones, e.g. failure to sit or crawl properly. Children may also be restless, excitable, collide with objects, fall over, eat messily, find difficulty in holding pencils or scissors, fail to engage in imaginative or creative play, fail to establish laterality and have language difficulties. Such pupils may avoid PE and games. By the time they reach secondary school they frequently have poor attendance.

Kirby, A. and Drew, S. (2002) *Guide to Dyspraxia and Developmental Co-ordination Disorders*. London: David Fulton Publishers.
Portwood, M. (1999) *Developmental Dyspraxia: Identification and Intervention: A Manual for Parents and Professionals* (2nd edn). London: David Fulton Publishers.
Ripley, K., Daines, B. and Barrett, J. (1997) *Dyspraxia: A Guide for Teachers and Parents*. London: David Fulton Publishers.

Contact

The Dyspraxia Foundation, 8 West Alley, Hitchin, Hertfordshire SG5 1EG. Tel: 01462 454986; Fax: 01462 455052; e-mail: dyspraxia@dyspraxiafoundation.org.uk; www.dyspraxiafoundation.org.uk

Early intervention

Early intervention is essential in ameliorating learning difficulties. The effective elements of early intervention include clear and direct instruction, intensive practice along with peer and adult support, positive feedback, treatment of any emotional and behavioural problems, differentiation of tasks, phonological awareness training, phonic decoding skills and liaison with parents/carers and external agencies. Other aspects include teaching based on a structured approach that sets targets, incorporates intensive practice along with formative assessment, and enables children to acquire independence and responsibility for their own learning.

Drifte, C. (2002) *Early Learning Goals for Children with Special Needs*. London: David Fulton Publishers.

Green, J. (2003) *Basic Skills for Childcare – Literacy*. London: David Fulton Publishers.

Green, J. (2003) *Basic Skills for Childcare – Numeracy*. London: David Fulton Publishers.

Meisels, S.J. and Shonkoff, J.P. (eds) (1996) *Handbook of Early Childhood Intervention*. Cambridge: Cambridge University Press.

Talay-Ongan, A. (1998) *Typical and Atypical Development in Early Childhood*. Leicester: BPS Books.

Early intervention strategies

Early intervention strategies for young children include gross motor activities (walking, throwing, catching, hopping, skipping and hoop games) and fine-motor activities (tracing, copying, using templates, water control, cutting with scissors and using pencil and paper). Specific strategies for improved auditory processing include phonological awareness training (using nursery rhymes and word games), listening to and identifying natural and recorded sounds, making sounds, discriminating between high and low and loud or soft sounds, following directions, repeating sentences and ordering events. Strategies for improving visual processing include using pegboard designs, using coloured wooden and plastic blocks, assembling puzzles, classifying objects, matching geometrical shapes and identifying missing objects.

Early signs

Early signs or precursors of learning difficulties can be difficulties with auditory processing (phonological awareness, discrimination, blending, sequencing, memory storage and recall), visual processing difficulties (discrimination and memory), speech and language difficulties (listening and communicating), attention and concentration (hyperactivity and impulsivity). Other problems include those affecting gross-motor skills (clumsiness) and fine-motor skills (dressing and using pencils pens). Early identification is necessary for both prevention and intervention. However, there can be problems with the process of early identification. Some children experience developmental lags that may disappear over time or when they mature. Labelling may create problems and low expectations may be a self-fulfilling prophecy. The early identification process for young children may be subject to errors due to psychometric issues such as the uncertain reliability and validity of assessment instruments. Children as a consequence may be under- or over-identified as having learning difficulties.

Emergent literacy

Emergent literacy refers to the pre-reading stage, that is those reading behaviours that precede literacy. This stage begins in the early years, and with children with learning difficulties it can extend into the primary years. Some children can learn and some do learn to read in the preschool years and this ability to read before attending school is related to learning opportunities and experiences. Preschool children can become aware of and interested in stories, books and print. Through these experiences they begin to learn about letters and words. Phonologically they become aware of rhymes and that some words commence with identical sounds. Some also develop phonemic awareness of sounds within words. Those preschool children who are more advanced are able to connect sounds and words with print. However, most children will need to be taught the skills and strategies for word recognition and comprehension and they will need opportunities to develop these skills and strategies. Children's awareness and interest in letters, words, sounds, rhymes, print and books need to be encouraged by adults and teachers. They will need support as well as encouragement to reach the goal of independence, especially if they lack phonemic awareness and word recognition skills.

Byrne, B. (1998) *The Foundation of Literacy: The Child's Acquisition of the Alphabetic Principle.* Mahweh, NJ: Lawrence Erlbaum Associates.
Westwood, P. (2004) *Reading and Learning Difficulties.* London: David Fulton Publishers.

Emotional and behavioural factors

Emotional and behavioural difficulties can be the cause or the effect of learning difficulties. It may be difficult to establish with certainty whether a particular child's learning difficulty is the result or the cause of a pre-existing emotional or behavioural problem. Children with emotional and behavioural problems often experience learning difficulties. Various kinds of emotional and behavioural difficulties, such as anxiety, depression, conduct disorders, ADHD and phobias, can adversely affect learning and contribute to or exacerbate learning difficulties. Children with these problems have difficulty in accessing the curriculum and, as a result, often underachieve or fail to achieve. They are also frequently absent from school or class and often lack the necessary social skills that contribute to success at school. Further information and strategies relating to emotional and behavioural difficulties can be found in the companion volume co-authored by Ayers and Prytys and listed below.

Ayers, H., Clarke, D. and Murray, A. (2000) *Perspectives on Behaviour: A Practical Guide to Effective Interventions for Teachers* (2nd edn). London: David Fulton Publishers.
Ayers, H. and Prytys, C. (2002) *An A to Z Practical Guide to Emotional and Behavioural Difficulties.* London: David Fulton Publishers.
Carr, A. (1999) *The Handbook of Child and Adolescent Clinical Psychology: A Contextual Approach.* London: Routledge.
Carr, A. (ed.) (2000) *What Works with Children and Adolescents.* London: Brunner-Routledge.
Emerson, E. (1995) *Challenging Behaviour: Analysis and Intervention in People with Learning Difficulties.* Cambridge: Cambridge University Press.
O'Brien, T. (1998) *Promoting Positive Behaviour.* London: David Fulton Publishers.

Epilepsy

A medical condition characterised by various types of seizures (tonic-clonic, atonic, myoclonic, complex partial or temporal lobe, and absence) that affects people of all levels of intelligence. Some people may discover that certain things or events trigger seizure, including lack of food and sleep, excitement and boredom. However, most seizures do not have an identifiable trigger. There may be changes in the course or pattern of seizures but these are not predictable. Some types of epilepsy are connected to brain injuries and it is likely that some people with brain injury experience both epilepsy and learning disabilities. Epilepsy and learning disabilities can be a part of certain syndromes, for example Tuberous Sclerosis. Some children with epilepsy experience learning and/or behavioural difficulties but it is not necessarily the case that these difficulties are related to epilepsy. Children with learning difficulties may also experience epilepsy.

Johnson, M. and Parkinson, G. (2002) *Epilepsy: A Practical Guide.* London: David Fulton Publishers.

Contact

Epilepsy Action, New Anstey House, Gate Way Drive, Yeadon, Leeds LS19 7XY. Tel: No. 0113 210 8800; Freephone Helpline: 0808 800 5555; E-mail helpline: help@epilepsy.org.uk; www.epilepsy.org.uk

Error analysis

In mathematics, error analysis is a method of identifying the different kinds of errors that pupils make in their computations. Appropriate and sufficiently large samples of work are required for error analysis to be valid and reliable. Sometimes the errors are systematic, at other times random. These errors may be due to incorrect steps in an algorithm or to problems with recall or even a consequence of distraction. There are many common errors including those pertaining to the number system (place value) and to algorithms (number facts). Error analysis can be useful in identifying particular problems but it can be time-consuming. It needs to be supplemented by interviews and discussions with pupils. Interviews enable teachers to identify error patterns and faulty problem-solving techniques as well as negative feelings and attitudes towards maths. Error analysis should lead not only to identification of pupil errors but also to reflection by teachers on their methods of instruction and delivery.

Ashlock, R.B. (1998) *Error Patterns in Computation: A Semi-programmed Approach*. (7th edn). Upper Saddle River, NJ: Merrill/Prentice-Hall.

Expectancy-value theory

This theory suggests that effort is dependent on children valuing tasks and outcomes and believing that they will achieve success. Children who are unconfident and who undervalue a task will not expend the necessary effort to achieve success. This is sometimes referred to as self-handicapping. A lack of confidence can be related to a lack of perceived self-efficacy, a lack of self-worth or a fear of failure. It can be the case that children would rather be seen as not making an effort rather than appearing unintelligent. Adults should be aware of this desire to protect self-worth in their approach to children with learning difficulties. Fear of failure can be as much an obstacle to learning as inadequate skills or knowledge.

Explanatory style

This occurs when people explain failure as being due to internal, global and stable factors or to external, specific and unstable factors. Internal factors include perceived lack of ability, lack of interest or poor attention. External factors include blaming teachers or learning materials. Global explanations include believing that all learning materials are unhelpful, whereas specific explanations could include the idea that particular learning materials are useless. Stable factors include the idea that one will always lack ability, whereas unstable factors could include the idea that one lacked ability on a particular occasion. Learners attributing failure to internal, stable and global factors are seen as more likely to be pessimistic about achieving success and will be easily discouraged and, as a result, experience failure.

Explicit teaching

Explicit or direct teaching is often recommended, particularly in the case of effective early intervention programmes. This type of teaching states clearly what skills are to be taught and what needs to be achieved. Children are provided with appropriate methods for dealing with their difficulties, are supported intensively during the learning process and are also provided with copious practice and positive feedback. Some of the elements of explicit teaching include providing learners with a range of strategies, providing guidelines that focus on improving concentration and also providing opportunities for learners to explain their decision-making with regard to learning processes.

Expressive language disorder

Expressive language is the process of producing speech. Children with expressive language disorders can understand the speech and language of other people but experience difficulties in speaking or talking. A number of disorders are connected to expressive language such as dysnomia, a difficulty with word finding or remembering or expressing words, and apraxia in which word sounds are remembered but they are unable to speak even though they do not have a paralysis. These disorders are not due to defects in speech muscles.

Owens, R.E. (1995) *Language Disorders: A Functional Approach to Assessment and Intervention.* New York: Merrill/Macmillan.

Extrinsic and intrinsic motivation

Extrinsic motivation is where learners attempt tasks in order to achieve rewards or to avoid the negative effects of failure. In some cases learners might need to be motivated by the use of rewards if they do not currently experience tasks as rewarding in themselves. Intrinsic motivation is when learners experience tasks as rewarding in themselves. Hopefully, learners will acquire intrinsic motivation but this can be assisted through extrinsic motivation, i.e. the use of rewards to encourage learners to become self-motivated and experience satisfaction through successfully completing tasks.

Failure

Internal and external factors can both contribute to learning failure. Internal factors include low ability, emotional and behavioural problems, medical syndromes or conditions, neurological problems, genetic influences, learning difficulties and disabilities, sensory impairment, low perceived self-efficacy, learned helplessness, fear of failure and motivational problems. External factors include inadequate or inappropriate teaching and teaching methods, lack of differentiation, inappropriate curriculum, negative teacher–learner relationships, truancy and absenteeism, and negative classroom or school environment. Some teachers tend to subscribe to a child-deficit model and ascribe failure solely to internal factors, usually low ability, or, alternatively, if they attribute failure to external factors they usually refer to poor parenting. These teachers may underestimate or ignore other external factors such as teaching methods or other teaching-related factors. It is more productive to consider an interactionist approach, the possible influence and interaction of both external and internal factors.

Feedback

Learners need frequent, continuous, positive and corrective feedback. The absence, inadequacy or negativity of feedback can adversely affect the motivation of learners leading them to avoid or to cease making an effort to attempt or complete tasks.

Forgetting

Learners with learning difficulties often experience problems with recall. Failure to remember can be due to a number of factors such as irrelevance or unimportance of information, inattention, decay or fading of information, conflicting information (proactive interference and retroactive inhibition), distractions and negative emotional states. In order to aid recall adults should encourage the use of effective study and memorisation skills and also use multi-sensory approaches to facilitate recall.

Formative assessment

Formative assessment involves the frequent evaluation of a pupil's performance in such a way that it enables teaching methods or materials to be changed or modified in order to improve that performance. Through formative assessment the teacher reflects on the effectiveness of their teaching style, methods, materials and delivery and modifies them, if necessary, in relation to their pupil's performance.

Fragile X syndrome

A genetic medical condition that is one of the most common hereditary causes of a range of cognitive impairments from learning disabilities with normal IQs to severe intellectual disabilities including autism. It affects boys more than girls and may not be diagnosed until middle childhood. The symptoms of this syndrome may include physical characteristics (long face, large protruding ears and testicles, double-jointed fingers, flat feet and heart murmurs), intellectual disability (IQ range of 60 to 70), learning difficulties (slow learning, delayed speech) and challenging behaviour (ADHD or ADD, stereotypical actions, sensory defensiveness, anxiety, tantrums, shyness and depression). This condition can be passed on by asymptomatic individuals, and in some families it is recurrent but in others it can miss several generations before reappearing. The cause of Fragile X syndrome is a genetic mutation on one of the X chromosomes. This mutation can be diagnosed through a DNA test that can also detect unaffected carriers of the mutation. The condition is under-diagnosed due in part to a lack of awareness among doctors and also to the variability of symptoms. There is no cure but help is available through specialised educational programmes addressing learning and behavioural difficulties, speech and occupational therapy and medication.

Sanders, S. (1999) *Fragile X Syndrome: A Guide for Teachers*. London: David Fulton Publishers.

G

Generalisation

Children with learning difficulties can experience difficulties in generalising learning from one context to another. Learners need to apply skills and knowledge to new situations or contexts. Adults need to consider ways of encouraging, facilitating and reinforcing generalisation by teaching how the same skills and knowledge can apply to different contexts.

Genetics

Behavioural genetics undertakes research into the effects of heredity on behaviour. The aim of genetics is to identify those medical conditions, disorders and disabilities that have an underlying genetic basis. Some conditions, disorders and disabilities run in families. This may be due to heredity or to the environment or to the interaction of both heredity and the environment. In order to uncover inherited conditions it is necessary to study twins, families and adopted children. Down's and Fragile X syndromes are examples of inherited conditions. Genetic factors are believed to play a part in SpLD, reading disability and also in ADHD. There is controversy in the field of behavioural genetics particularly over the relative contributions of heredity and the environment to the determination of intelligence and behaviour.

Ceci, S.J. and Williams, W.M. (eds) (1999) *The Nature–Nurture Debate: The Essential Readings*, Oxford: Blackwell.

Clark, W.R. and Grunstein, M. (2000) *Are We Hardwired? The Role of Genes in Human Behavior*. Oxford: Oxford University Press.

Lewontin, R.C. (1993) *The Doctrine of DNA: Biology as Ideology*. London: Penguin.

Plomin, R., DeFries, J.C., McClearn, G.E. and Rutter, M. (1997) *Behavioral Genetics* (3rd edn). New York: W.H. Freeman.

Rose, S., Kamin, L.J. and Lewontin, R.C. (1984) *Not In Our Genes: Biology, Ideology and Human Nature*. London: Penguin.

Group work

Placing pupils with learning difficulties in well-managed and well-organised small groups is seen as an effective way of bringing about teaching and learning. Pupils with similar learning needs are placed in the same group. However, flexibility is retained to meet changing needs. Small groups are particularly useful for pupils learning basic skills. They encourage pupils to participate, enable teachers to provide more feedback and to more easily monitor pupil performance, and also enable pupils to progress at rates commensurate with their capabilities. In order for small-group work to be effective, rules for small-group work should be established; pupils in the group should be similar in skills and abilities, the groupings should be flexible and the location of the group should be free from distractions and disruptions. Rigid ability grouping should be avoided because it may adversely affect the motivation of pupils with learning difficulties. There is a danger of group work being unplanned and disorganised, simply ending up as pupils working separately in a group setting.

Guided reading

Guided reading is where teachers guide pupils into adopting appropriate strategies for accessing particular texts. The guidance may take the form of teaching word identification and decoding skills, vocabulary and, in particular, comprehension strategies for accessing unfamiliar texts. It is intended for pupils in their third or fourth year at school and is delivered in three stages: before, during and after reading. The before reading stage builds on pupils' background knowledge, encouraging questions and predictions about the text, and expanding vocabulary. The during reading stage is where teachers encourage pupils to think up questions, identify causal relationships and main ideas, read critically and make comparisons and contrasts. The after reading stage encourages pupils to retell, summarise, reflect and evaluate. These sessions are intended to encourage the pupil to be an active learner who participates in discussions, shares ideas and engages in co-operative learning. Through guided reading, teachers are able to identify and assess a pupil's reading comprehension strategies, and in the light of that to modify their approach to guided reading.

Blair-Larsen, S.M. and Williams, K.A. (eds) (1999) *The Balanced Reading Program*. Newark, DE: International Reading Association.
Fountas, I.C. and Pinnell, G.S. (1996) *Guided Reading*. Portsmouth, NH: Heinemann.

Handwriting

Poor handwriting is often due to poor learning and inadequate teaching but it can also be due to a difficulty with fine muscle control and poor hand–eye co-ordination. Handwriting should be taught early in a child's school career. Children with handwriting difficulties need intensive practice and clear instruction as poor handwriting restricts development. Many handwriting difficulties are due to poor sitting posture, inappropriate pencil grip and paper placement, or an inadequate teaching of letter formation.

Taylor, J. (2001) *Handwriting: A Teacher's Guide: Multisensory Approaches to Assessing and Improving Handwriting Skills.* London: David Fulton Publishers.

Health

Various types of health problems can affect learning due to their physical and psychological impact. Health problems may cause pain and discomfort affecting concentration. Children with health problems may be on medication that may also affect concentration and effort. In some cases children with learning difficulties can simulate illness so they can avoid certain lessons or avoid specific tasks, particularly reading, or they may avoid school generally. In other cases children develop psychosomatic disorders associated with particular teachers or the school environment. Lack of adequate or inappropriate nutrition and insufficient sleep may also affect children's concentration and energy.

Closs, A. (ed.) (1999) *The Education of Children with Medical Conditions.* London: David Fulton Publishers.

Home environment

This can affect learning through socio-economic deprivation, for example through overcrowding, lack of space or a room for homework, lack of books and other learning materials and no available computer. In the home there may be a lack of support and encouragement from parents and siblings, distractions in the form of TV, computer games and noise, family conflict and stress, or poor parental physical and mental heath. Some children may possess resilience and may be able to cope with these negative influences and still achieve success.

IEP (Individual Education Plan)

A support plan for a pupil with special educational needs that is provided through the revised SEN Code of Practice. It is for a pupil that is not making any or sufficient progress. This plan sets out individualised targets to meet the specific needs of the named pupil. The plan identifies the pupil's stage of development, strengths and weaknesses, resources available, the interventions that address the pupil's needs, the success criteria for those interventions and a review date. This process is known as School Action.

Cornwall, J. and Robertson, C. (1999) *IEPS – Physical Disabilities and Medical Conditions*. London: David Fulton Publishers.

Cornwall, J. and Tod, J. (1998) *IEPS – Emotional and Behavioural Difficulties*. London: David Fulton Publishers.

Tod, J. (1999) *IEPS – Dyslexia*. London: David Fulton Publishers.

Tod, J. and Blamires, M. (1998) *IEPS – Speech and Language*. London: David Fulton Publishers.

Tod, J., Castle, F. and Blamires, M. (1998) *IEPS – Implementing Effective Practice*. London: David Fulton Publishers.

Inadequate teaching

Inadequate teaching means using inappropriate teaching methods, providing insufficient teaching time, inappropriate learning materials and ineffective support. It can, especially in the early years, contribute to learning difficulties.

In-class support

This is provided by specialist teachers, teaching assistants or learning mentors. It is usually one-to-one support, in particular classes or lessons assisting and helping pupils with special educational needs to access the National Curriculum. In-class support can have negative effects if it embarrasses the pupil or makes him/her feel inadequate. Pupils can feel stigmatised and even rejected, and as a consequence avoid support altogether. Schools need to be careful how they provide in-class support to avoid labelling and stigmatising SEN pupils.

Inclusion

The Warnock report (DES 1978) described three types of integration, namely locational, social and functional. In locational integration children are placed in units within a mainstream school with no, or little, contact with mainstream peers. In social integration pupils mix socially but for most of the time are educated apart from mainstream pupils. In functional integration all pupils, whatever their difficulties, are placed in mainstream classes.

The term inclusion refers to pupils with emotional and behavioural difficulties and/or learning difficulties/disabilities being included in or attending mainstream schools and mainstream classes. Many of these children will have received a statement and will receive in-class and/or withdrawal support from a specialist support teacher, a learning mentor or teaching assistant. The topic of inclusion is controversial, particularly with regard to children with emotional and behavioural difficulties. Some believe that children with learning difficulties should attend special schools in order to take advantage of smaller classes and groups and a specially adapted curriculum, and also to benefit from trained and experienced teachers in learning difficulties. Others believe that children with learning difficulties benefit from sharing the facilities of mainstream schools and classes and from engaging with the mainstream curriculum as well as enjoying social integration with their peers. In mainstream schools children with learning difficulties may not receive individualised or personalised support from adequately trained and experienced teachers/teaching assistants and may miss out on the specialised facilities and amenities that exist in special schools. However, mainstream schools can provide individualised in-class and withdrawal support, this support being provided by specialist teachers or by teaching assistants. Mainstream schools are also in the position to provide a broader curriculum and greater resources. The inclusion of pupils with learning difficulties in mainstream schools can also be a learning experience for mainstream pupils and teachers, enabling them to experience those children's problems and leading to greater understanding and tolerance. The use of assistive technology can also support the inclusion of pupils in mainstream schools. There is a growing tendency to include children with a variety of learning difficulties or children who have, as a component of their special educational needs, a learning difficulty or difficulties. This tendency has led to the closure of special schools and the inclusion of their pupils into mainstream schools. However, special schools may be in a position to develop collaborative partnerships with mainstream schools. Some parents appeal against inclusion of their children into mainstream schools for the reasons given above. Additional arguments opposing inclusion are that curricular and subject differentiation will not actually be implemented in mainstream schools, that the necessary planning will not take place, that specialist resources will be unavailable or will be inadequate, mainstream teachers will be largely untrained and inexperienced in special needs, and also unmotivated, that pupils will experience stigmatisation and labelling and feel inferior, and finally, that it can be physically unsafe.

Babbage, R., Byers, R. and Redding, H. (1999) *Approaches to Teaching and Learning: Including Pupils with Learning Difficulties*. London: David Fulton Publishers.

Cheminais, R. (2003) *Closing the Inclusion Gap: Special and Mainstream Schools Working in Partnership*. London: David Fulton Publishers.

Clark, C., Dyson, A. and Millward, A. (eds) (1995) *Towards Inclusive Schools?* London: David
  Fulton Publishers.
DES (1978) *Special Educational Needs* (The Warnock Report). London: HMSO.
Farrell, P. (1997) *Teaching Pupils With Learning Difficulties: Strategies and Solutions.* London: Cassell.
Kenward, H. (1997) *Integrating Pupils with Disabilities in Mainstream School: Making it Happen.*
  London: David Fulton Publishers.
Lorenz, S. (2002) *First Steps in Inclusion: A Handbook for Parents, Teachers, Governors and LEAs.*
  London: David Fulton Publishers.
Stakes, R. and Hornby, G. (2000) *Meeting Special Needs in Mainstream Schools: A Practical Guide
  for Teachers.* London: David Fulton Publishers.

Intellectual disability

A child with intellectual disabilities has an impaired cognitive ability. Pupils in this
category display limited cognitive ability and below-average competence in academic,
linguistic and social functioning. Although these children have intellectual disabilities it
is still possible for them to achieve some success in learning. The severity of intellectual
disability is categorised as mild, moderate, severe and profound. Each category is described
in terms of a range of IQ. The mild category commences with an IQ of below 70. The
focus currently is not so much on IQ but rather on a pupil's existing strengths and
weaknesses. The focus is also on the required resources and support to enable learning to
progress. The mild category is within the IQ range 70 to 55. These pupils can usually
acquire basic literacy and numeracy skills but are below-average in achievement. The
moderate category is within the range 40 to 55. These children will need a high level of
support through school and into adult life. The severe category is from 25 to 40 and
the profound category is below 25. These children frequently have additional problems
with regard to visual and auditory perception, mobility and communication. They may
also have health problems and medical conditions. Children with severe and profound
disabilities need high levels of support throughout their lives. Behavioural techniques are
used to train these children to acquire eating, washing, toileting and dressing skills. These
techniques can also be used to address the challenging behaviours that can occur such as
temper outbursts, physical aggression, self-injurious behaviour and obsessive-compulsive
rituals. Other useful techniques include approaches that stimulate sensory awareness
and help develop existing reflexes and responses. Some children with intellectual disability may display symptoms of autism or autistic spectrum disorder. The type of autism
displayed by children with an intellectual disability is one characterised by unusual repetitive actions or behaviour and is often associated with self-injury. The factors contributing
to intellectual disability include hereditary factors such as in Down's syndrome or Fragile
X syndrome; prenatal factors such as substance abuse, rubella, premature birth and
toxicity; perinatal or postnatal factors such as birth complications or brain injury;
and environmental factors such as malnutrition. In many instances it is not possible to
identify a specific factor.

In terms of teaching children with intellectual disability it is necessary to make content meaningful and relevant, to secure and maintain attention, to improve retention through frequent practice and revision and to effect generalisation through repeatedly teaching the same skills and knowledge in different contexts. Motivation can be increased through positive reinforcement for effort as well as for achievement. With regard to language these children will require stimulation and direct instruction and in severe cases they will need alternative methods of communication such as sign language or symbol communication. In terms of social development, social skills training is necessary so that they can relate to other children and reduce or eliminate those negative behaviours that may contribute to rejection and isolation. In general, teaching should be based on using real situations as well as direct instruction to promote learning.

Gates, B. (ed.) (2003) *Learning Disabilities: Toward Inclusion* (4th edn). London: Churchill Livingston.
Lerner, J.W. (2003) *Learning Disabilities* (9th edn). Boston, MA: Houghton Mifflin.
Westwood, P. (2004) *Learning and Learning Difficulties: A Handbook for Teachers*. London: David Fulton Publishers.

Intelligence

There are various definitions and models of intelligence. There are also controversies over definitions and models of intelligence and the extent to which intelligence is genetically and/or environmentally determined. One view sees intelligence as relatively fixed whereas another view sees it as relatively fluid due to the influence of learning and experience. The fixed view states that there is an upper genetically predetermined limit for any given individual, but the other view believes that teaching and learning can increase an individual's intelligence. A teacher's view of the nature of intelligence can influence their teaching of particular pupils or groups of pupils. Teachers holding the view that intelligence is relatively fixed may feel pessimistic about the possibility of significant academic progress for their pupils and, as a result, limit or restrict their teaching goals. Teachers holding an environmental view may be over-optimistic about what given pupils can achieve and, as a consequence, have unrealistic expectations. It would seem best to avoid both a fatalistic and an over-optimistic view of a given pupil's academic potential and think about what type of appropriate teaching and learning can lead that particular pupil to fulfil his/her potential.

Ceci, S.J. (1996) *On Intelligence* (2nd edn). Cambridge, MA: Harvard University Press.
Cooper, C. (1999) *Intelligence and Abilities*. London: Routledge.
Deary, I.J. (2001) *Intelligence: A Very Short Introduction*. Oxford: Oxford University Press.
Gould, S.J. (1997) *The Mismeasure of Man* (2nd edn). London: Penguin.

Intervention programmes

Effective interventions include task analysis, simple and clear instructions, consistent monitoring, intensive practice, peer tutoring, visual presentations, the use of alternative resource materials, computer-assisted programmes, pupil active participation, the use of calculators and individualised or personalised support and small-group work. Early intervention is recommended in order to prevent learning difficulties occurring or to prevent them from becoming serious. The general characteristics of early intervention include direct and explicit teaching, teaching specific skills and strategies, intensive practice, corrective and positive feedback, positive reinforcement, appropriate differentiation of methods and material, addressing emotional and behavioural problems, using peer and parental/carer support and liaison with external agencies. Pupils may require individualised or personalised, intensive one-to-one in-class support or withdrawal to a small group.

Teaching methods should include a relatively fast-paced delivery, a range of presentations, guided practice, strategy training, pupil participatory activities, scaffolding and formative assessment.

IQ

IQ tests such as the Wechsler Intelligence Scale for Children (WISC-IV) are used to determine levels of intelligence or ability, and therefore academic potential. As with the concept of intelligence there are controversies surrounding intelligence tests and intelligence testing. Questions have been raised regarding what they actually measure, their accuracy, their fairness and whether other measures would be more useful in determining a pupil's potential. It has also been stated that IQ tests are not diagnostic in terms of providing information for educational planning and that although correlating with academic achievement in school they do not always accurately predict the progress of a particular pupil. As regards learning difficulties, IQ tests have been used as a basis for determining the discrepancy between a pupil's achievement and ability. This discrepancy is quantified through a discrepancy formula. There is controversy about the use of discrepancy formulae in terms that their use is based on failure or 'wait and fail', and they emphasise the criterion of underachievement rather than other components such as psychological factors or phonological problems. Criticisms have been made in relation to the use of IQ tests with children with learning difficulties. Pupils with learning difficulties find it difficult to adjust and respond in the testing context because of physical, sensory, language, communication, attentional and behavioural difficulties. The IQ score does not relate to a pupil's performance levels in terms of basic skills and the curriculum and therefore does not provide the necessary information for individualised teaching and learning programmes for those pupils. Finally, IQ is not necessarily a fixed entity, as pupil IQ scores can undergo change and, as a result, decisions made on the basis of a fixed IQ may not be valid.

Farrell, P. (1997) *Teaching Pupils with Learning Difficulties: Strategies and Solutions.* London: Cassell.

Kamin, L.J. (1977) *The Science and Politics of IQ.* London: Penguin.

Kline, P. (1998) *The New Psychometrics: Science, Psychology and Measurement.* London: Routledge.

Mackintosh, N.J. (1998) *IQ and Human Intelligence.* Oxford: Oxford University Press.

Murphy, K.R. and Davidshofer, C.O. (1998) *Psychological Testing: Principles and Applications* (4th edn). Englewood Cliffs, NJ: Prentice-Hall.

Knowledge acquisition

Pupils with learning difficulties may experience a lack of automaticity in retrieving factual knowledge or in being able to perform a series of procedures. Pupils lacking automaticity spend an inordinate amount of time in recalling information or in remembering procedures.

Language

Language assumes a variety of forms – oral (listening and speaking), reading and writing. Children who lack phonological or phonemic awareness need practice with language sounds. Phonological experiences establish the basis for word-recognition skills. Phonological awareness refers to a child's ability to use the sounds of language in spoken words. Children who have reading difficulties are not tuned in to the phoneme sounds of language and words. Beginner readers must be aware of phoneme sounds within words. The alphabet will be inaccessible if children do not perceive the sounds within words. There is a correlation between inadequate phonological awareness and poor reading in many alphabetically based languages. Phonological awareness can be taught and facilitates reading.

Griffiths, F. (2002) *Communication Counts: Speech and Language Difficulties in the Early Years*. London: David Fulton Publishers.
Martin, D and Miller, C. (2002) *Speech and Language Difficulties in the Classroom* (2nd edn). London: David Fulton Publishers.

Language delay

Language delay occurs when children are failing to acquire speech and language at the appropriate time. These children are behind the normal milestones for language acquisition. In some cases children never develop speech and have to rely on alternative communication skills.

Language disorders

These disorders encompass all forms of communication including delayed speech, problems with vocabulary, the meanings of words and the formation of concepts. Other disorders encompass the misuse of grammar and syntax and poor comprehension. Many pupils with learning difficulties have a language problem. Some pupils have a disorder in listening and some have language delay. Children with the medical condition *otitis media* (infection of the middle ear causing hearing loss) have impaired language learning. Compared with normal readers, poor readers have less verbal fluency, smaller vocabularies, less syntactical ability and manifest difficulties with semantics and phonology. Receptive language disorders include those where children cannot understand a single word, cannot understand sentences or may understand a word in one context but not another. Children may repeat words or sentences without understanding a disorder called echolalia. Some children experience a lack of tone discrimination, cannot discriminate or blend single-letter sounds and are unable to recognise small word parts (morphemes) within a sentence.

Expressive language disorders are where children depend on gestures in order to communicate. They are unable to speak or talk. There are difficulties in remembering and expressing words. Children may remember the sound of a word but cannot use their voice to make the correct sounds even though they do not have paralysis. In other cases children can speak in single words or phrases but have difficulty with constructing sentences.

Language and language skills

The assessment and interventions for language difficulties require teachers to be familiar with phonology (system of rules for sounds and sound combinations – phonemes), morphology (morphemes – roots and affixes), syntax (system of rules for combining words and morphemes for grammatically correct sentences), semantics (language meaning) and pragmatics (social use of language influencing actions and attitudes). There can be various deficits in respect of these categories. Phonological deficits can appear as articulation problems, such as omitting consonants, or as reception problems, such as difficulties in discrimination. Morphological deficits include not using appropriate inflectional endings in speech. Syntactical deficits include not using appropriate age-related sentence constructions, problems in comprehending sentences that express relationships, inferences, questions, mood or negation. Semantic deficits include using and understanding a restricted vocabulary, failing to perceive multiple meanings, failing to understand the figurative use of language and failing to comprehend logical relationships and verbal analogies. Pragmatic deficits include failing to answer questions appropriately, failing to adapt speech to a listener's needs, entering into conversation inappropriately, failing to stay on topic and difficulties in interpreting verbal and non-verbal cues. The assessment of language skills is through formal tests and informal methods.

Listening skills can be taught through the following strategies. Phonological awareness training (activities to facilitate perception and recognition of phonemes), building a listening vocabulary (teaching nouns, adjectives and adverbs), understanding sentences (through directions, identifying pictures), comprehension (directions, pictorial stories, detailed questioning), critical listening (recognising absurd stories) and listening to stories (reading stories along with detailed questioning).

Language skills can be taught through using natural opportunities to expand a child's language, through parallel talk and through self-talk. A speaking vocabulary can be constructed through naming objects and asking for missing words and for word combinations.

Learned helplessness

This concept was formulated by Seligman as a way of describing the expectations of helplessness and lack of control that were generalised to new situations after experiencing exposure to situations from which there was no possibility of escape or avoidance. Continual exposure to academic failure contributes to learned helplessness, avoidance, withdrawal, lack of persistence and unwillingness to attempt new learning tasks. Pupils with learning difficulties can adopt an attitude of learned helplessness. They can be passive learners unwilling or reluctant to accept responsibility for their own learning. They may lack persistence and be unwilling to attempt new tasks. They may also see themselves as generally unsuccessful learners who, when successful, attribute any success to luck rather than effort or ability. Teachers and parents can help to prevent learned helplessness by praising their children's successes, by not attributing failure to a lack of ability and by not being overly concerned about the odd mistake.

Seligman, M. (1975) Helplessness: *On Depression, Development and Death*. San Francisco, CA: W.H. Freeman.

Learning difficulties

The term 'learning difficulty' is normally applied to pupils who are not making sufficient progress particularly in basic skills such as literacy and numeracy. The prevalence of such difficulties depends on definitions. The SEN Code of Practice defines children as having learning difficulties if they have difficulties in learning that are greater than most children in their age group, and if they have difficulties which prevent them from using educational facilities in a school or LEA. A specific learning difficulty refers to pupils who have learning difficulties even though they have at least average intelligence, do not have sensory impairments or health problems, do not have emotional or behavioural problems, do not experience deprivation and have accessed the curriculum and been appropriately taught. There is a discrepancy between intelligence, or ability, and achievement. Specific learning difficulties include dyslexia, dyscalculia and dyspraxia. Intellectual disability refers to children whose ability or intelligence is below average and which affects their functioning in terms of academic, psychological, physical, social and general adaptation to their environment. This intellectual disability is divided into mild, moderate and severe. The causes of intellectual disability include genetic, prenatal, perinatal, postnatal and environmental factors.

Aird, R. (2001) *The Education and Care of Children with Severe, Profound and Multiple Learning Difficulties*. London: David Fulton Publishers.
Lerner, J.W. (2003) *Learning Disabilities* (9th edn). Boston, MA: Houghton Mifflin.
Westwood, P. (2004) *Learning and Learning Difficulties: A Handbook for Teachers*. London: David Fulton Publishers.

Learning styles

It has been stated that a certain type of learning style can contribute to learning difficulties. This learning style is one where there is poor concentration, passivity, distractibility, impulsivity and inadequate self-monitoring and self-correction. However, it could be the case that a poor learning style may be the effect rather than the cause of failure. Whether it is the cause or effect of a particular learning style, it is helpful to improve learning through cognitive interventions including that of metacognitive training.

Riding, R. (2002) *School Learning and Cognitive Style*. London: David Fulton Publishers.
Riding, R. and Rayner, S. (1998) *Cognitive Styles and Learning Strategies*. London: David Fulton Publishers.

Learning theories

There are various learning theories that have implications for learning difficulties. The most common ones include behavioural, cognitive, cognitive-behavioural and constructivist theories. Behavioural theory encompasses classical and operant conditioning, the use of behaviour analysis and behavioural teaching. Cognitive theory encompasses information processing and cognitive schemata. Cognitive-behavioural theories, including social learning theory, encompass modelling, perceived self-efficacy, locus of control, attribution, metacognition, self-regulation and motivational style. Constructivist theories are based on a process-centred approach and incorporate the ideas of scaffolding and the zone of proximal development.

Schunk, D.H. (2003) *Learning Theories: An Educational Perspective*. (4th edn). Upper Saddle River, NJ: Prentice-Hall.
Westwood, P. (2004) *Learning and Learning Difficulties: A Handbook for Teachers*. London: David Fulton Publishers.

Locus of control

This refers to what individuals perceive as controlling their behaviour, not what in reality may actually be controlling their behaviour. This control is seen as lying along a continuum from high external to high internal. Individuals who have high internal accept responsibility for their learning and behaviour, whereas those who are high external attribute their success or failure to external factors. Pupils with learning difficulties who have an external locus of control are inclined to attribute their lack of success to external factors such as bad luck or poor teaching.

Long-term memory

Pupils with learning difficulties can have poor concentration, poor attention and also be poor at encoding information into long-term memory. They may also be poor at retrieving that information and lack memory-improving strategies to address memory difficulties. The following strategies can help with retrieval of information in long-term memory: organisational schemes such as using word webs and using pre-existing knowledge to establish linkages.

Malnutrition

Pre- and postnatal malnutrition can affect neurological and cognitive development. In the early years inadequate nutrition can affect IQ, attention, memory and achievement. It is stated that nutrition can affect mood, concentration and effort in learning.

Mathematical difficulties

Failure to acquire basic mathematical skills and concepts in the primary school will lead to children being unable to develop a foundation for future development in secondary and tertiary education. Frequent failure will lead to loss of confidence and motivation and an avoidance of the subject. Many factors are believed to contribute to failure to learn basic skills and concepts – perceptual and motor problems, developmental delay, absenteeism, inadequate teaching and anxiety. A specific learning difficulty in mathematics is called dyscalculia. This specific learning difficulty affects mathematical skills in a child who is otherwise normal in terms of intelligence and education. Pupils with severe reading difficulties can also experience difficulties in mathematics. However, there are some pupils who do not have reading and writing difficulties but who do have difficulties with mathematics. Mathematical difficulties at secondary level include basic arithmetical operations, fractions, decimals, percentages, place value and mathematical language and terminology. Secondary-age pupils need to be presented with copious worked examples, plenty of practice problems of different kinds and explicit instruction.

The causes of mathematical difficulties have been attributed to internal deficits, in particular deficits, in cognitive processes such as symbolic understanding, memory difficulties, poor concentration and problems with auditory discrimination. Additionally, acute and chronic anxiety over learning maths has been quoted as an internal factor contributing to mathematical difficulties and the avoidance of mathematics altogether. Others have focused on the nature and quality of the teaching of mathematics as a cause of mathematical difficulties. Some see maths teaching as not relating directly to children's experiences and others that it is too preoccupied with teaching arithmetical operations to the exclusion of problem-solving techniques.

Berger, A., Morris, D. and Portman, J. (2000) *Implementing the National Numeracy Strategy for Pupils with Learning Difficulties: Access to the Daily Mathematics Lesson.* London: David Fulton Publishers.

Bley, N.S. and Thornton, C.A. (1995) *Teaching Mathematics to Students with Learning Disabilities* (3rd edn). Austin, TX: ProEd.

Booker, G., Bond, D., Briggs, J. and Davey, G. (1997) *Teaching Primary Mathematics* (2nd edn). Melbourne: Addison-Wesley Longman.

Donlan, C. (ed.) (1998) *The Development of Mathematical Skills*. Hove: Erlbaum.

Heddens, J.W. and Speer, W.R. (1995) *Today's Mathematics Concepts and Classroom Methods* (8th edn). Columbus, OH: Prentice-Hall.

Lerner, J. (2003) *Learning Disabilities* (9th edn). Boston, MA: Houghton Mifflin.

Mercer, C. D. and Mercer, A.R. (1993) *Teaching Students with Learning Problems* (4th edn). New York: Merrill.

Miles, T.R. and Miles, E. (1992) *Dyslexia and Mathematics*. London: Routledge.

Reys, R., Suydam, M., Lindquist, M. and Smith, N. (1998) *Helping Children Learn Mathematics* (5th edn). Boston, MA: Allyn & Bacon.

Westwood, P. (2000) *Numeracy and Learning Difficulties: Approaches to teaching and Assessment*. London: David Fulton Publishers.

Maths anxiety

Maths anxiety or phobia refers to negative emotional reactions to mathematics causing individuals to avoid or reject the learning of mathematics and to freeze when confronted by mathematics in the classroom. Similarly, maths anxiety also appears at the time of mathematics tests. Children with learning difficulties can experience this type of anxiety.

Buxton, L. (1991) *Math Panic*. Portsmouth, NH: Heinemann.

Metacognition

A reflective cognitive process where one is aware of and has knowledge of one's own thinking and reasoning and its underlying basis. With regard to learning, it refers to a process of self-reflection where learners plan, monitor and modify their thoughts and actions as they execute particular tasks. This process is where learners reflect on and think about their own thinking and reasoning processes in order to improve their learning strategies. It is believed that learning difficulties can be exacerbated and even caused by a lack of metacognitive strategies.

Metacognitive training

This training aims at improving metacognitive strategies of children with learning difficulties. Metacognitive strategies are taught by using direct teaching and modelling methods. Teachers speak about and demonstrate particular strategies. Pupils are then encouraged to observe teachers, think and talk about those strategies themselves and to transfer and generalise them to different contexts. Pupils are also encouraged to reflect on and monitor their use of strategies. This also involves pupils engaging in self-instruction and self-questioning in order to develop self-confidence and motivation to attempt and complete tasks. Metacognitive strategies include classification (reflection on the nature and significance of the task), checking (about progress and outcome), evaluation (about quality of outcome) and prediction (about possible options and outcomes).

Meta-memory

Meta-memory refers to people's awareness of their own specific memory processes such as recall, retrieval and storage of information. Some pupils with learning difficulties will need to become more aware of their memory processes and strategies for improving recall, retrieval and storage of information. Pupils with learning difficulties experience problems with attention, retrieval and long-term memory.

Miscue analysis

An approach to assessing oral reading. Miscues are errors that pupils make while reading orally. These miscues are seen as diagnostic opportunities through which pupils reveal their underlying language structures and processes.

Motivation

Learning difficulties are often seen as being exacerbated by a lack of motivation. Motivation can often be regarded as a trait rather than a state. When motivation is viewed as a trait it is also seen as being innate and therefore not amenable to change or to being influenced by external factors. Seeing motivation as unchangeable leads to pessimism and therefore to an unwillingness to try and improve teaching. However, motivation can be influenced by internal factors such as beliefs, expectations and attributions and by external factors such as positive reinforcement, individualised support or a change in the curriculum. Changing these factors may well motivate pupils to become more fully engaged in attempting and completing tasks. There are two types of motivation: intrinsic and extrinsic. Intrinsic arises from personal satisfaction arising from the task or activity itself whereas extrinsic is due to receiving rewards or avoiding negative consequences. In order to increase motivation it is helpful to encourage rather than criticise; make the curriculum appropriate, interesting and relevant; provide opportunities for pupils to exercise some control and make choices; provide group work; and give positive feedback and rewards for effort as well as attainment.

Motivational style

Children with learning difficulties can often display a negative or maladaptive motivational style. This style is characterised by a fear of failure, learned helplessness, avoidance of work and avoidance of seeking help. It can also take the form of self-handicapping.

Motor skills learning

Motor skills include gross motor skills, involving the large muscles for posture, walking and running. They also include fine motor skills, involving small muscles for co-ordination of hands and fingers and dexterity with speech and tongue muscles. Many motor skills are acquired through modelling and trial and error. However, motor skills in school need to be taught and practised so they can be performed automatically. New motor skills are best taught through modelling and direct instruction and strengthened by positive feedback and by encouraging pupils to self-correct their own performances. Gross motor skills development can be encouraged through play, playing games and other physical activities. Fine motor skills can be encouraged through tracing and stencils, water control, using scissors, paper-and-pencil activities and copying activities.

Multi-sensory environment

A multi-sensory environment is a specially designed environment that enables children with profound and multiple learning difficulties to activate devices that produce sounds and visual effects. The aim is to stimulate responses and also to provide a relaxing environment. A room that has this type of environment is called a sensory stimulation room.

Pagliano, P. (2001) *Using a Multisensory Environment: A Practical Guide for Teachers*. London: David Fulton Publishers.

Multi-sensory teaching

Multi-sensory methods use different senses to reinforce learning such as visual, auditory, kinaesthetic and tactile. These methods include characteristics such as providing links with visual, auditory, kinaesthetic and tactile senses; using phonics instruction; providing frequent practice and repetition; and using sequential lessons that practise explicit teaching.

Naming-speed deficits

Some children experience problems with rapid automatic naming or word finding. These children find it difficult to name objects and are slow in finding correct words. Slowness in naming or word finding is due to poor recall and retrieval and restricts the development of a sight vocabulary and the decoding of unfamiliar words.

National Literacy Strategy

Children who have learning difficulties may be responsive to normal teaching strategies or they may have needs that require different strategies. Children with severe and complex learning difficulties will require different types of work and different approaches. During the Literacy Hour children with learning difficulties will be expected to participate either for the entire time or for at least a part of it; however, extra support may be required, either in class, or outside class, but parallel to the Literacy Hour itself. Some children may require additional or special materials. It is an opportunity to focus on phonics, vocabulary, spelling and writing. Children may be grouped according to their needs within the classroom, enabling a teaching assistant or mentor to provide focused support. The effectiveness of the National Literacy Strategy depends on high expectations and target setting. Class work should be connected to the objectives set out in IEPs. IEPs should state the steps necessary to meet those objectives, the resources needed and the adult support required.

Berger, A. and Gross, J. (eds) (1999) *Teaching the Literacy Hour in an Inclusive Classroom*. London: David Fulton Publishers.

Noise and learning

Noise levels in classrooms can be due to internal noise such as off-task pupil-generated noise (shouting, scraping furniture, drumming on desks, fidgeting and making animal-like sounds) or to external noise (road traffic, aircraft and building works). Noise can distract pupils, particularly those who are easily distractible such as pupils with ADD/ADHD.

Observational learning

Learning through imitation or by copying the performance, actions or behaviour of others. It can be incidental – that is learning through a chance opportunity – or intentional – that is through teachers creating opportunities for observational learning. This type of learning requires the pupil to be attentive to the teacher, retentive of observed knowledge and skills, to recall and imitate actions and behaviour and to be motivated to learn. Children with learning difficulties can lack concentration, fail to retain information or reproduce skills, and lack motivation, so making it difficult for them to learn through observation.

On-task behaviour

Behaviour where pupils are actively engaged in concentrating on various aspects of a lesson. These aspects include teacher instructions and presentations, lesson materials, appropriate use of lesson equipment and positive interactions with other pupils. Children with learning difficulties can find it difficult to be on-task if the lesson presentation, explanation, task and materials are too difficult or if there are distractions. Teachers can encourage on-task behaviour through appropriate teaching methods, differentiation of delivery and materials and through the use of behavioural teaching and behavioural management.

Operant conditioning

An element of behavioural teaching and behavioural management. Learning or behaviour that is positively reinforced or rewarded tends to be repeated. The focus is on using positive reinforcement such as using descriptive praise, smiles, privileges and tokens to increase or strengthen the performance of pupils with learning difficulties. Positive reinforcement is contingent or dependent on pupils making the correct behavioural or learning responses.

Orthographic units

Pronounceable parts of a word such as -ing, -dem, -in, -pro. These groups of letters provide cues for word recognition and word meaning without needing to know each letter or each word. Sight recognition of orthographic units, the use of contextual cues and the decoding of words indicate pupils' increasing level of reading skills.

Overlearning

Overlearning is a type of learning where pupils keep on practising even when they have reached a point where they appear to have achieved adequate competence levels. Retention and retrieval is made easier by overlearning and it is particularly helpful for learning difficult concepts and skills.

Paired reading / writing

An approach to providing reading / writing support and can be undertaken by parents/ carers, pupils, teaching assistants and mentors, as well as teachers. The teacher and the pupil read a book together. The pupil chooses the book. Both read the first page or pages together at the pupil's pace. If the pupil makes a mistake the teacher points at the word and repeats it correctly. Pupils are praised when they attempt to read and when they actually read sentences and paragraphs independently. If the pupil comes across an unfamiliar word the teacher waits a few seconds, and if the pupil is incorrect the teacher supplies the word and the pupil then repeats it. This approach is interactive, with discussion and questioning occurring during and after reading. This approach leads to improvements in pupils' reading ages.

Radinski, T. and Padak, N. (2000) *Effective Reading Strategies: Teaching Children Who Find Reading Difficult* (2nd edn). New York: Merrill.

Topping, K. (1995) *Paired Reading, Writing and Spelling: A Handbook for Teachers and Parents.* London: Cassell.

Parents

A positive relationship between schools and parents/carers of pupils with learning difficulties is essential and is best expressed in a parent–school partnership. Parents should take an active role in their children's education, be aware and have knowledge of their children's entitlement, have access to and be incorporated in the assessment process and be involved in decision-making with regard to SEN provision and support. Parents request and require early identification and assessment of their children's difficulties, clear, non-judgemental and unambiguous decisions from professionals, advice on support, participation in parents' support groups and contact with specialist organisations. Parents should also receive information that enables them to arrive at informed judgements about their children's needs. Parents can provide support through encouraging and rewarding their children's efforts and achievements and by providing help with homework and preparations for school. Schools should consult parents, listen to their concerns and involve them in the assessment process and in planning IEPs. It can sometimes happen that parents do not support or show interest in their children's learning difficulties. This may be due to the parents' own learning difficulties or negative experiences of school. Other factors affecting parental interest include social and economic deprivation, stress, fatigue, physical illness, psychological and psychiatric disorders and family conflict. These parents need advice, support and encouragement from schools and from appropriate organisations and services.

Blamires, M., Robertson, C. and Blamires, J. (1997) *Parent–Teacher Partnership: Practical Approaches to Meet Special Educational Needs*. London: David Fulton Publishers.
Gascoigne, E. (1995) *Working with Parents as Partners in Special Educational Needs*. London: David Fulton Publishers.
Wolfendale, S. (ed.) (1997) *Working with Parents of SEN Children after the Code of Practice*. London: David Fulton Publishers.
Wolfendale, S. (ed.) (2002) *Parent Partnership Services for Special Educational Needs: Celebrations and Challenges*. London: David Fulton Publishers.

Pause, Prompt, Praise (PPP) strategy

This teaching strategy has been developed by Glynn and colleagues and is used when listening to children read. It is a strategy that can be used by parents, peer-tutors and helpers, as well as teachers. The teacher pauses or allows the pupil a few seconds to read an unfamiliar word and if the pupil fails to read the word the teacher prompts the pupil. If the pupil reads the word then the teacher praises the pupil. If, however, the pupil fails to read the word, even after prompts, then the teacher immediately supplies the word. If the pupil corrects a word while reading, the teacher praises the child. This strategy when used with decoding and phonics has brought about increases in the reading age of children.

Glynn, T., McNaughton, S., Robinson, V. and Quinn, M. (1979) *Remedial Reading at Home*. Wellington: New Zealand Council for Educational Research.

Peer group pressure

Peer groups can have negative effects on pupils with learning difficulties. Peers may exert negative pressure by focusing negative attention on them, by labelling or stigmatising them, or by distracting or diverting them from learning.

Peer tutoring

An approach where pupils work together on reading or writing. One pupil is the tutor and the other pupil is the learner. The pupils work in pairs. The peer tutor helps the tutee to learn, practise or evaluate their reading or writing skills. There are various models of peer tutoring including same-age and across-age tutoring. Both pupils benefit from peer tutoring, the tutor from teaching skills and the tutee from learning skills. The tutor can also model positive behaviours and facilitate social relationships in the classroom. Peer tutoring is an effective learning strategy and also supports inclusion.

Cole, P. and Chan, L. (1990) *Methods and Strategies for Special Education*. New York: Prentice-Hall.

Perceptual difficulties

Visual perception is necessary for learning basic skills, particularly accurate visual processing of letters, words, numbers and mathematical symbols. Some pupils with dyslexia do have visual processing difficulties, but not all. Deficits in visual and visual motor skills are not considered primary causes of learning difficulties except in a minority of children with learning difficulties and in the cases of children with brain damage or injuries.

Phonemic awareness

This term refers to an aspect of phonological awareness, that aspect which identifies and recognises that spoken words are made up of particular sounds. Children need training in phonemic awareness in order to identify phonemes within words. Absence of phonemic awareness means that children will be unable to recognise and discriminate speech sounds and therefore be unable to learn phonics. Phonemic awareness is seen as a powerful predictor of future reading ability and its absence as a possible factor in explaining reading disability. Phonemic awareness may be acquired naturally through listening to stories and reciting rhymes. Different aspects of phonemic awareness include identifying initial sounds, alliteration and, in particular, blending or combining phonemes to form words and segmenting words into phonemes.

Adams, M.J., Foorman, B.R., Lundberg, I. and Beeler, T. (1998) *Phonemic Awareness in Young Children: A Classroom Curriculum*. Baltimore, MD: Brookes.

Snow, C., Burns, S. and Griffin, P. (1998) *Preventing Reading Difficulties in Young Children*. Washington, DC: National Academy Press.

Stanovich, K.E. (2000) *Progress in Understanding Reading: Scientific Foundations and New Frontiers*. New York: Guilford Press.

Westwood, P. (2004) *Reading and Learning Difficulties*. London: David Fulton Publishers.

Phonic skills

The skills necessary to enable a learner to use their knowledge of letter–sound relationships in order to read and spell words. These skills are important in the early stages of reading and writing. Experienced readers use decoding strategies in reading unfamiliar words. It needs to be understood by learners that some speech sounds are represented by groups of letters and that the same sound may stand for more than one group of letters. Some recommend that beginners are taught how to recognise letter groups rather than decode from individual letters, for example by decoding words from onsets and rimes, e.g. black where bl = onset and ack = rime. Currently, the idea is to teach and relate phonics to relevant interesting and meaningful texts.

Phonics

The relationship between printed letters (graphemes) and sounds (phonemes). Children need to decode print, translate print into sounds and to learn the alphabetical code of the symbol–sound relationship. Children with learning difficulties need explicit teaching or direct instruction in the symbol–sound relationship. Before learning phonics children need to possess phonological awareness, the recognition that speech can be broken down or segmented into phonemes or sounds. Phonics teaching is effective in helping to prevent, as well as to treat, reading difficulties, particularly in the early years. However, some teachers may not have had phonics training themselves and may lack the foundations from which to teach phonics to children. There are various approaches to phonics including synthetic, analytic and analogical phonics. Synthetic phonics teaches children to explicitly translate letters into sounds (phonemes) and then blend the sounds to produce words. This approach requires the child to have good auditory discrimination, good blending skills and good retrieval of basic sound–symbol relationships. Analytic phonics teaches children to analyse and identify letter–sound relationships in sight words and then break down these words into sounds and letters. Children need the same kind of preliminary skills for analytic phonics that are necessary for synthetic phonics and for analogical phonics. Except with analogical phonics, a learner needs the ability to process, store and retrieve orthographic patterns. Analogical phonics teaches children to recognise rime segments or syllables of unfamiliar words as being the same as those in familiar words. The phonics approach has been criticised for boring children, for being decontextualised, and therefore impeding transfer and generalisation, and for being too distant from reading texts for meaning. Historically and currently, there is controversy over the contribution of phonics approaches to reading and spelling. However, it is now believed that phonics teaching is necessary for the early stages of learning to read but that it must be contextualised and be not simply a process of drills and practice. The teaching of phonics is best achieved through explicit and systematic teaching, through decontextualised tasks and activities, through conveying its usefulness and being used to assess a child's level of knowledge.

Cunningham, P. (2000) *Phonics They Use: Words for Reading and Writing* (3rd edn). New York: Longman.

Strickland, D.S. (1998) *Teaching Phonics Today: A Primer for Educators*. Newark, NJ: International Reading Association.

Westwood, P. (2004) *Reading and Learning Difficulties*. London: David Fulton Publishers.

Phonological awareness

Understanding of words as separate speech units, ability to detect differences and similarities of sounds, to break up words into separate sounds and to blend sounds into words. It is essential that children develop a high level of phonological awareness and, in particular, the acquisition of word concept, meaning that a child understands that a word is a unit of speech. Children need to develop a level of phonological awareness that enables them to benefit from teaching of letter–sound correspondences. With respect to dyslexia the current focus is on difficulties with phonological awareness and rapid automatic naming. Dyslexic pupils and others with reading difficulties have severe problems with the phonological elements of decoding, phonemic awareness and with the alphabetic principle. Some pupils also have problems of rapid naming with numbers and letters. This slow recall is a major problem in developing a sight vocabulary and rapid retrieval of letter–sound correspondences.

National Reading Panel (2000) *Teaching Children to Read: An Evidence-based Assessment of the Scientific Research Literature on Reading and Implications for Reading Instruction.* Washington, DC: National Institute of Child Health and Human Development.
Westwood, P. (2004) *Reading and Learning Difficulties.* London: David Fulton Publishers.

Phonological awareness training

Children who are learning to read need to become aware of the sounds in words and language. Phonological awareness training aims to use various strategies to train children to become aware of these sounds. These strategies include learning to count the sounds in words, segmenting the sounds and syllables in words and recognising rhyming words. Various activities that can increase phonological awareness of language sounds include getting children to listen to and identify slight changes in the names of common words, to clap out syllables in names and words, using nursery rhymes, rhyming words, riddles and games, adding, subtracting and deleting sounds.

Burnett, A. and Wylie, J. (2002) *Soundaround: Developing Phonological Awareness Skills in the Foundation Stage.* London: David Fulton Publishers.
Lerner, J.W. (2003) *Learning Disabilities* (9th edn). Boston, MA: Houghton Mifflin.

Portage scheme

A home-based scheme that helps preschool children with SEN who experience learning difficulties. It is named after Portage, Wisconsin, where it was developed. It is a scheme that encourages a partnership between parents and professionals enabling parents to work with their child using a behavioural approach. A Portage member visits parents and shows them how to set objectives and complete the Portage Checklist, a norm-referenced developmental checklist. This checklist can be used for programme planning. The objectives are broken down into steps using task analysis. Teaching activities or tasks are suggested using behavioural principles, and the progress made in relation to these tasks is then recorded and reviewed.

Contact

National Portage Association (NPA), PO Box 3075, Yeovil, Somerset BA21 3JE. Tel/Fax: 01935 471641; e-mail: npa@portageuk@uk.freeserve.co.uk; www.portage.org.uk

Portfolio assessment

This form of assessment collects samples of a pupil's work over a period of time. The portfolio of work is then used to evaluate the pupil's current achievement level and progress to date. It could include samples of daily work, tests, checklists, written stories, writing drafts at various stages, subject projects and observations. The teaching aims of the particular programme of tasks and activities should guide the choice of samples.

Poverty

Many children experiencing socio-economic deprivation tend to have lower school achievement compared to those children who are not experiencing deprivation. However, there are those resilient pupils and families who manage to achieve, educationally, even though they are experiencing deprivation. Children from deprived backgrounds may lack experiences in literacy and numeracy in the home. Home language may be different from that of the school and parental involvement and aspirations may be low. Teachers should not be pessimistic and deterministic with regard to children from a deprived background. With deprived children early intervention, structured programmes and parental support can help to surmount social and economic barriers.

Practice

Practice is essential in order for learning to take place and for learning to become fixed in the memory. Practice is most effective when it occurs periodically rather than at one single time. Practice leads to the development of automaticity, an essential element in learning. There are two main kinds of practice, independent and guided. Guided practice is where a pupil's performance is closely monitored with immediate, positive and corrective feedback. Independent practice is where pupils work without constant monitoring and frequent feedback.

Precision teaching

A behavioural teaching approach based on the use of probes, criterion-referenced tests, task analysis, objectives, specific targets, regular (that is daily) measurement and the graphic representation of pupil's attainment levels through daily record sheets. Regular measurement enables teachers to evaluate the effectiveness of interventions and to effect appropriate changes.

Lindsley, O. (1992) 'Precision teaching: discoveries and effects'. *Journal of Applied Behaviour Anaysis*, **25**(1), 21–6.

Prevalence

Prevalence refers to the number of cases of a difficulty, disability or disorder in a particular population over a specified period. Prevalence rates vary depending on definitions, assessment and diagnostic criteria, and they may also vary across schools and countries. Factors affecting prevalence rates include age, gender, ethnicity, medical interventions and socio-economic variables. Prevalence rates can also be affected by under- or over-identification of the difficulty or disorder. Prevalence rates have a direct bearing on educational planning and the allocation of resources. The term 'incidence' refers to the number of new cases in a given population over a specified period.

P-scales or levels

P-scales are performance indicators or assessment criteria for children with SEN for progress below Level 1 in the NC programmes of study. They have been developed for children between the ages of 5 and 16 and are intended to help with target setting through summative assessment at the end of the key stages. However, for some pupils who make more rapid progress they can be used once a year. There is a P-scale for each National Curriculum subject. The scales are divided up into eight levels, P1 being the lowest and P8 the highest. From summer 2005, the DfES will request schools to report the achievement of SEN pupils working below Level 1 as a P-level.

Berger, A., Buck, D. and Davis, V. (eds) (2001) *Assessing Pupils' Performance Using the P Levels*. London: David Fulton Publishers.

Psychomotor skills

Skills that are necessary for a variety of motor activities. Those activities involve using hands, feet, mouth and brain to perform co-ordinated actions or behaviours. Some motor skills are acquired through observation and modelling but most in the school context require direct instruction along with positive and corrective feedback. Motor skills need to be practised regularly in order to become automatic.

Questioning strategies

Questioning strategies are used to stimulate the thinking processes of pupils who are engaged in reading activities. Questioning should be planned so as to stimulate explanation, evaluation and judgement. Examples of questioning strategies are: asking for literal comprehension of the text; interpretations of the text; and critical and creative readings of the text. Self-questioning strategies are those that pupils develop for themselves and consist of them asking themselves questions about the text.

R

Rating scales

Assessment scales used to record observations and measurement of a pupil's progress. They can be used as the basis for judgements about pupils with learning difficulties.

Readability level

Readability of a given text refers to the level of reading skill that is required in order to read the text. Readability affects reading fluency. A text should be at the readability level of the pupil. If a given text has too many unfamiliar or difficult words then fluency will be adversely affected. An independent reading level requires that at least 97 per cent of the words should be identifiable. If less than 90 per cent of words are identifiable then a frustration level is reached. It is a good idea for teachers to read to pupils when pupils have reached their frustration level. This will help pupils improve their knowledge of comprehension and sentence structure and expand their vocabulary.

Reading assessment

Reading assessment aims at identifying a pupil's reading ability, strengths and weaknesses, measuring progress, making comparisons between pupils and screening pupils. Assessment is also seen as the basis for choosing appropriate teaching methods and programmes. There are different philosophies in the area of reading assessment, namely the testing of specific skills approach (sight vocabulary, phonics, blending, decoding and comprehension) and the holistic approach based on observations of readers interacting with texts. Assessment strategies include structured observation, checklists, informal reading inventories (graded samples), running records (miscue or error analysis), dynamic (adapting and modifying strategies according to responses) and pupil interviews (cognitive, attitudinal and emotional factors). Diagnostic testing includes testing of phonic knowledge, decoding skills, phonemic awareness and word recognition. Another approach to assessment is benchmarking. Sight vocabulary can be assessed through a word list, decoding skills through checklists, self-correction through running records and comprehension through pupil interviews.

Leslie, L. (1997) *Authentic Literacy Assessment: An Ecological Approach*. New York: Longman.
Mariotti, A. and Homan, S. (2001) *Linking Reading Assessment to Instruction* (3rd edn). Mahwah, NJ: Erlbaum.

Miller, W.H. (1995) *Alternative Assessment Techniques for Reading and Writing*. West Nyack: NY Centre for Applied Research in Education.

Reading comprehension

The ability to extract meaning from texts. For many pupils with learning difficulties the main problem is comprehension of texts. Word recognition skills do not necessarily evolve into comprehension skills. Many such pupils acquire word recognition skills but many continue to struggle with comprehension. In order to improve comprehension skills it is helpful to teach the appropriate vocabulary prior to reading the text, to increase the background knowledge brought to the text, to encourage a problem-solving approach to the text and to encourage active interaction with the text. Comprehension strategies include monitoring comprehension, use of graphic and semantic organisers, questioning and self-questioning, story structures and summaries. Particular strategies include directed reading-thinking activity (DRTA); Know–Want to know–Learned (KWL); the 3H strategy (Here–Hidden–In My Head); and Preview–Question–Read–Summarise (PQRS).

Vacca, J.A., Vacca, R.T. and Gove, M.K. (2000) *Reading and Learning to Read*. New York: Longman.
Walker, B.J. (2004) *Diagnostic Teaching of Reading* (5th edn). Upper Saddle River, NJ: Pearson Merrill.
Westwood, P. (1997) *Commonsense Methods for Children with Special Needs* (3rd edn). London: Routledge.
Yopp, R.H. and Yopp, H.K. (2001) *Literature-Based Reading Activities* (3rd edn). Boston, MA: Allyn and Bacon.

Reading difficulties

These include inadequate word recognition and poor decoding skills. Reading fluency and reading for meaning are adversely affected by weaknesses in word recognition. Inadequate fluency can lead to a lack of motivation, resistance to reading activities and a desire to avoid reading tasks. There are many factors that may contribute to reading difficulties. Some are within-child factors, some are in-school factors and some are in-home factors. Within-child factors include cognitive (low ability), neurological, linguistic, perceptual, emotional, behavioural and motivational factors. In-school factors include poor teaching, inappropriate teaching methods and materials, insufficient allocation of time and support, unsupportive classroom environment and negative peer pressure. In-home factors include lack of parental interest and support, lack of space, distractions, and parental and family stress and conflict. These factors do not necessarily preclude children from achieving reading success. Children may be resilient and overcome these factors and succeed in reading. Therefore it is worthwhile for teachers and parents/carers to adopt an optimistic outlook even though some of these factors may be present.

Carver, R.P. (2000) *The Causes of High and Low Reading Achievement*. Mahwah, NJ: Erlbaum.

Clay, M.M. (1985) *The Early Detection of Reading Difficulties*. Auckland, NZ: Heinemann.

Lerner, J.W. (2003) *Learning Disabilities*. Boston, MA: Houghton Mifflin.

Westwood, P. (2004) *Reading and Learning Difficulties: Approaches to Teaching and Assessment*. London: David Fulton Publishers.

Reading Recovery

Reading Recovery is an early intervention approach developed in New Zealand by Marie Clay. This approach is used in the UK and is targeted at children who display reading and writing difficulties after the first year of school. The aim is to address reading difficulties before they adversely affect motivation and confidence. The focus is on intensive reading and practice for a period of about fifteen weeks or until they reach their class average. They receive individualised, intensive and direct teaching in daily sessions of 30 minutes duration with a trained Reading Recovery teacher. Sessions focus on word recognition and reading comprehension strategies. A variety of activities are included in the sessions such as writing brief stories, working with plastic letters to form words, sentence construction with word cards, reading a new book or re-reading a familiar book to the teacher. Books are carefully graded so as to enable progression from simpler to more difficult texts. Teachers are trained to identify the readability levels of texts and to make running records of children's reading performances. It is believed to be an effective approach in increasing the level of children's reading performances. However, it is expensive, dependent on specialist teachers and some claim that the achieved improvement is not maintained over time and does not generalise to classroom contexts.

Clay, M.M. (1994) *A Guidebook for Reading Recovery Teachers*. Portsmouth, NH: Heinemann.

Reading strategies

Reading strategies include those for improving word recognition (teaching phonological awareness and using phonics methods), those for increasing fluency (repeated reading and use of basal readers), those for improving background knowledge (language experience and KWL method), those for expanding vocabulary (providing concrete experiences with words, collecting new words, classifying and categorising words and using graphic organisers and the cloze procedure).

Reception language disorders

The process of understanding spoken language is called oral receptive language and a disorder of this process is a receptive language disorder. Some children cannot understand any words whereas others have problems with sentences and phrases. A child with a disorder may understand individual words but have difficulties with understanding sentences.

Some understand a word in one context but not in others. Another type of disorder is echolalia, the repeating of words or sentences without understanding their meanings. Some children are unable to blend or isolate letter sounds and others are unable to discriminate morphemes within words.

Martin, D. and Miller, C. (2002) *Speech and Language Difficulties in the Classroom* (2nd edn). London: David Fulton Publishers.

Reciprocal teaching

This approach requires the teacher and the pupil to reciprocate through sharing the reading, questioning and interpretation of texts. It is based on learning as a social activity, as a dialogue between teachers and pupils and the teacher's role as one of mediation and the nature of assessment as being a dynamic process. The approach follows four steps: the first step is the teacher reading the text; the second step sees the teacher explaining and modelling out aloud the strategies of clarifying, questioning, predicting and summarising; the third step consists of pupils with support reading out aloud a different text; and the final step consists of pupils demonstrating the strategies. It is an effective approach to teaching learning strategies and encourages learners to actively participate rather than being passive.

Palinscar, A.S. and Brown, A.L. (1984) 'Reciprocal teaching of comprehension-fostering and monitoring activities'. *Cognition and Instruction*, **1**, 117–75.

Reinforcement

A major element in the behavioural approach to teaching. It is based on the principle that people will increase a given behaviour if they are positively reinforced for its performance. This approach can be applied to learning as well as behaviour. In the case of pupils with learning difficulties positive reinforcement can be used to increase on-task behaviour, effort and achievement. The teacher should identify material (stars, certificates, tokens) and non-material (praise, smiles) positive reinforcers or rewards appropriate for their pupils. The reinforcers should motivate their pupils and increase their learning performance. The teacher should identify pupil responses that will trigger the reinforcers. They should also modify the classroom environment so that pupils receive reinforcement for learning. Reinforcement should be increased or decreased depending on a positive or negative learning performance.

Remedial support

There are three basic approaches to remedial support: in-class support, withdrawal to a resource room and a combination of both. In-class support is provided by a specialist teacher, a teaching assistant or learning mentor, usually supporting an individual pupil or a group of pupils with learning difficulties. Withdrawal support is where a pupil, or pupils, is withdrawn and taught separately in a resources room.

There are various advantages and disadvantages of the approaches. Both models depend on support from teachers or teaching assistants that have sufficient knowledge and skills to support pupils effectively. Sometimes this is not the case. Withdrawal support can be based on a restricted curriculum, repetition of worksheets and lead to discontinuities in teaching and learning and to a paucity of instruction in learning strategies. Furthermore, withdrawal can disrupt classroom and teaching routines, divest mainstream teachers of their responsibilities for pupils with learning difficulties, stigmatise pupils and lead to a lack of co-ordination between mainstream and remedial teachers. The focus is now on inclusion within schools and also within mainstream classrooms. However, in-class support, unless adequately planned and implemented, can be affected by some of the same difficulties that affect withdrawal support. Pupils with learning difficulties in mainstream classes or lessons can be stigmatised, receive inadequate teaching, be provided with undifferentiated learning materials and experience distractions from and disruption by other pupils. The model of withdrawal in combination with in-class support is one that would appear to combine the advantages of both.

Resilience

An attribute that enables individuals to reduce or even eliminate the influence of factors that could adversely affect their learning and behaviour.

Children with learning difficulties may possess this quality of resilience enabling them to preserve their self-esteem and self-confidence even though they experience adversity.

Resource rooms

A resource room is a separate classroom or space where pupils with learning difficulties are withdrawn for intensive learning support provided by teachers, teaching assistants, mentors or helpers. This support is usually provided once or twice a week for an individual or a small group of pupils. The resource room model has been criticised for isolating and stigmatising pupils, for deskilling mainstream teachers and for not providing the full curriculum. However, pupils in a resource room can receive intensive individual tuition in an environment that is free from distraction and disruption.

Resource teachers

The resource teacher, if adequately trained and motivated, can provide support for mainstream teachers by offering advice, co-planning lessons and IEPs (targets, strategies and resources), co-teaching, providing INSET, and contacting and consulting external agencies. The role of the resource teacher is now seen as more consultative and collabora-tive than previously, when he/she was seen as simply a teacher who supported pupils in a resource room.

Retrieval

Retrieval is recalling or remembering information that has been stored in the long-term memory. Information needs to be retrieved from the long-term memory and placed in the working or short-term memory. There are two types of memory: episodic memories (of events), and semantic memories (of concepts, knowledge and language). Strategies for improving storage and retrieval include organising schemes such as word webs and building on prior or previous knowledge.

Rote-learning

A learning process that is dependent on committing material to memory through drill and repetition. Criticisms of rote learning include the following: it does not promote understanding; it does not draw on background knowledge; it does not facilitate easy recall or retrieval; it is easily forgotten and it does not generalise to different contexts. However, some aspects of memorisation are useful in learning basic factual information, in accessing core materials and in processes leading to higher-level cognitive skills and learning strategies. Memorisation can be useful and necessary where lower level cognitive processes need to be committed to memory. However, memorisation must be linked to meaningful and relevant material.

Running records

Running records are useful for identifying pupils who need learning support. They are based on observation of a pupil's responses. A pupil's responses can be a guide to his/her knowledge and use of learning strategies. The main aim of running records is planning learning support. The validity of running records depends on pupils' learning responses being an accurate and representative sample of their performance. With regard to read-ing, running records can be used to record the main indicators of reading performance including accuracy, fluency and self-correction.

S

Scaffolding

Scaffolding support refers to teachers supporting pupils in the early stages of learning a task. This form of support is based on Vygotsky's idea of the zone of proximal development. The teacher sets a task at a level that is not too easy and not too difficult. The task should be sufficiently challenging to motivate the learner and to build upon and extend the pupil's existing level of knowledge, competence or performance. Types of scaffold include modelling, guiding, thinking through and mediation. Reciprocal teaching is a type of scaffolded instruction.

School Action and School Action Plus

School Action and School Action Plus are laid out in the SEN Code of Practice (DfES 2001). In School Action a class or subject teacher, together with the SENCO, identifies a pupil as having learning difficulties and, as a result, formulate and implement interventions that address those difficulties. School Action Plus occurs where the pupil has not made sufficient progress as a result of School Action. The class or subject teacher and the SENCO will arrange a review meeting with the parent/carer. This may involve discussion over whether to refer the pupil to external agencies, e.g. the Educational Psychology Service.

Scotopic sensitivity or Irlen syndrome (tinted lenses)

Refers to a syndrome or difficulty with processing light efficiently enough to be able to read. The treatment recommended is the use of tinted lenses and coloured overlays to eliminate sensitivity to light. The treatment is controversial. However, some individuals claim an improvement in reading.

Screening

The screening process attempts to identify children who need further investigation for learning difficulties. It is a process that assesses children's visual and aural perception, speech and language, motor skills and cognitive and social development. Screening interviews and questionnaires are used to identify those children who are likely to experience learning difficulties. The aim of early detection is early intervention.

Second language learners

Children who are second language learners are often over-represented in special education. This can be due to being misidentified as children with learning difficulties. It can be difficult to separate out or disentangle English language needs from learning difficulties. Children who are second language learners can have difficulties with comprehension, vocabulary, grammar and fluency. Other problems include deficiencies in phonological awareness and sight vocabulary. These learning barriers can also restrict social communication with other children, further inhibiting language development.

Hall, D., Griffiths, D., Haslam, L. and Wilkin, Y. (2001) *Assessing the Needs of Bilingual Pupils: Living in Two Languages* (2nd edn). London: David Fulton Publishers.

Self-concept

Self-concept refers to one's concept of oneself in its totality. Self-esteem has an evaluative component that connects to one's perceived degree or level of self-worth, that is how one values oneself. Children with a negative self-concept can perceive themselves as lacking the ability, the skills and the confidence to learn. They can become passive learners, unwilling and reluctant to make the effort to learn, and feeling that whatever they do they will inevitably experience failure. Holding a negative self-concept can contribute to learning difficulties or exacerbate existing learning difficulties.

Self-correction

This occurs when a child realises a mistake has been made and then self-corrects. The rate of self-correction can be quantified through running records and an increase in self-correction can be seen as a sign that the child is improving and becoming more independent in their reading. The self-correction rate can be used as a motivational device. Where the child is failing to self-correct it is necessary to point out to the child the usefulness of noticing errors and self-correcting.

Self-esteem

Children with learning difficulties can experience low self-esteem or low self-worth. It can take many forms including refusal to learn, hostility, resistance to instructions, dependency, passivity, discouragement, frustration, avoidance and withdrawal. Pupils with learning difficulties feel insecure and inept and as a consequence experience low self-esteem. However, not all pupils experience low self-esteem, some display resilience and are able to maintain their self-esteem. Pupils who experience success in other areas of the curriculum and have the respect and support of their peers may well maintain their self-esteem. Parents, carers and teachers can help build positive self-esteem through providing guidance and support to enable children to feel in control of their learning. Children should learn to identify the causes of their success and failure so they avoid blaming themselves and others. Instead they should concentrate on making efforts to produce positive outcomes and develop coping mechanisms and strategies that will address failures. Teachers can use clinical teaching to help build self-esteem. Clinical teaching requires teachers to develop a genuine rapport with their pupils, to encourage their pupils to contribute to analysis of their difficulties and evaluation of their performance. It is important to have high but realistic expectations of learning potential and to provide positive reinforcement and positive feedback contingent on effort and performance. Teachers are also required to ensure that the work is structured and organised in the form of routines that contribute to success and that pupils are aware of and value their success. It helps to provide pupils with tasks that encourage the acceptance of responsibility and that enable them to feel mature. The possibility of success increases when pupils are provided with material that is relevant and interesting. Reading texts that help pupils to understand themselves and their problems can contribute to successful learning experiences for those pupils. Attribution retraining is another way of building self-esteem. This requires pupils to be retrained from attributing their poor performance to external locus of control factors (bad luck or difficult work) to attributing their poor performance to internal locus of control factors (lack of effort and lack of strategies). The focus of attribution retraining is to encourage pupils to attribute their failure to lack of effort and to the lack of strategies. Teachers should provide pupils with reinforcement and positive feedback for effort and for the use of appropriate learning strategies.

Barrow, G., Bradshaw, E. and Newton T. (2001) *Improving Behaviour and Raising Self-Esteem in the Classroom: A Practical Guide to Using Transactional Analysis.* London: David Fulton Publishers.
Lawrence, D. (1987) *Enhancing Self-Esteem in the Classroom.* London: Paul Chapman.

Self-handicapping

Refers to various strategies adopted by children in order to avoid feelings of failure. These strategies include the avoidance of learning tasks altogether, making insufficient effort and not seeking support when it is necessary.

Self-injurious behaviour

Self-inflicted, repetitive behaviour that causes physical harm to the afflicted child or adolescent. It can take different forms such as biting, head banging, gouging and hair pulling. It can occur among those who experience severe learning difficulties. Possible reasons for self-injury include seeking attention, avoidance and self-stimulation. Behaviour modification techniques are used to address self-injurious behaviours.

Emerson, E. (1995) *Challenging Behaviour: Analysis and Intervention in People with Learning Difficulties*, Cambridge: Cambridge University Press.

Self-monitoring

Self-monitoring is a strategy where children learn to check their own responses and errors. This strategy requires active participation in the learning process. Children are taught how to stop, listen and look before responding to a difficulty. The aim of self-monitoring is to reduce impulsive and unreflective responses to learning difficulties.

Sensory impairment

Impairments in sight and hearing can have a bearing on learning difficulties. When children experience learning difficulties it is necessary to eliminate sensory impairment factors. Pupils who have impaired hearing find it difficult to acquire grammar and vocabulary and to access audio-vocal methods. Deaf pupils' reading, writing and spelling abilities are often delayed. Visual impairment can lead to delays in perception and concept formation, motor skills, visual functioning and emotional difficulties.

Mason, H. and McCall, S. (eds) (1997) *Visual Impairment: Access to Education for Children and Young People*. London: David Fulton Publishers.

Separate classes

Separate classes for pupils with learning difficulties are usually small in numbers and consist of pupils with different types of learning difficulties. Pupils may benefit from separate classes by receiving more attention and more intensive instruction and by avoiding the distractions and disruption apparent in some mainstream classes. With a lower teacher–pupil ratio, individualised teaching and differentiation, progress is more likely than in some mainstream classes and lessons where pupils may not experience these benefits. In separate classes pupils may increase on-task behaviour and may be more likely to complete set tasks.

Shaping

Shaping is a behavioural teaching method where approximations to a desired answer or response are positively reinforced or rewarded until the desired response is achieved.

Shared book experience

SBE is a teaching method designed to establish the basis for reading. The approach is usually used during the first year of school but can also be used with older children. Learning is perceived as a social experience, therefore small group participation and co-operation is encouraged. The aim is to encourage interest and enjoyment of books, to develop concepts of print, to develop phonemic and syntactical awareness, to use contextual cues and to develop word recognition skills and comprehension skills. With SBE, children have stories read to them using books that excite interest and comment. The stories are read with enthusiasm and with normal fluency in order to engage children's interests. After the story has been read, children are asked questions and asked for their comments. The questions encourage prediction, interpretation and criticism as well as factual comments. During the second and subsequent readings, children are encouraged to read alongside the teacher or parent in a way that encourages word recognition, decoding and the use of contextual cues.

Holdaway, D. (1990) *Independence in Reading* (3rd edn). Sydney: Ashton Scholastic.

Short-term memory

This is where information is consciously stored, temporarily, for a very short period of time. This type of memory can be adversely affected by anxiety, depression and stress. Certain types of drugs may also affect short-term memory.

Sight vocabulary

A collection of words a child should know by sight, that is instantly and without hesitation. Fluency in reading requires a sight vocabulary. A basic sight vocabulary usually refers to a hundred or more commonly occurring words, many of these words being acquired through visual memory. Frequent exposures to sight words help store the orthographic patterns of those words in long-term memory. When the words are met again they are immediately identified through perception of letters within the words. Children with learning difficulties need to acquire sight vocabulary as a matter of priority. The accumulation of sight words improves automaticity. Approaches to teaching sight vocabulary include the use of flash cards, writing the words while speaking them out aloud and various games and activities.

Fields, M. and Spangler, K.L. (2000) *Let's Begin Reading Right* (4th edn). Upper Saddle River, NJ: Pearson Merrill.
Talbot, V. (1997) *Teaching, Reading, Writing and Spelling*. Thousand Oaks, CA: Corwin Press.

Silent sustained reading

SSR is where children are given the opportunity to read silently and regularly for a given period of time in the classroom. Problems with this approach include children choosing inappropriate books, either too easy or too difficult, and that children secretly avoid reading. This approach, to be effective, requires intensive monitoring to ensure on-task behaviour.

Skills-based approach

An approach to reading based on three methods, namely synthetic phonics, analytic phonics and analogic phonics. A skills-based approach requires explicit direction and instruction on the part of the teacher.

Social constructivist theory

This approach emphasises the active and socially based construction of learning and understanding on the part of all learners. Learning is not something that is simply passed along or down to learners but rather a process they construct for themselves in collaboration with others. This approach encourages pupil-centred, collaborative, co-operative, group-based and problem-solving processes. The teacher's role is that of a facilitator who provides pupils with opportunities for exploratory and discovery activities. For children with learning difficulties this approach is best considered after basic skills have been acquired through direct teaching. Children with learning difficulties often require a structured approach where instructions are clear and strategies are taught. However, children, after acquiring basic skills and strategies, can build on this foundation through discovery, exploratory and problem-solving activities.

Selley, N. (1999) *The Art of Constructivist Teaching in Primary School*. London: David Fulton Publishers.

Social learning theory

This theory sees learning as the result of modelling or imitation. It is observational learning that is acquired through observing the responses or behaviour of other people. Positive or negative responses are learned through such imitating. Powerful, competent, skilled or respected role models are often those most likely to be imitated. Through observational learning, cognitive skills, language skills, learning strategies and problem-solving skills can be acquired. Seeing whether and how others are positively reinforced for their responses can also influence the responses of individuals. This is called vicarious learning. Children with learning difficulties may imitate or model themselves on positive or negative role models in terms of their attitudes and approaches to learning. Children develop ideas about their own perceived self-efficacy and their perceived levels of competence. Children with learning difficulties can experience negative self-efficacy, believing they lack the necessary ability and skills to achieve success and, as a result, are reluctant to engage with learning tasks. Self-efficacy is influenced by positive or negative criticism, by too-easy or too-difficult tasks and by the learner's own beliefs and expectations. Positive self-efficacy is encouraged through positive reinforcement of effort as well as achievement and through setting realistic, achievable targets and tasks.

Bandura, A. (1977) *Social Learning Theory*. Morristown, NJ: General Learning.
Bandura, A. (1997) *Self-Efficacy: The Exercise of Control*. New York: Freeman.

Social skills difficulties

Children with learning difficulties may lack social skills or not use the social skills they have acquired. Social skills include understanding social situations, sensitivity to the feelings of others, responding appropriately to social cues, adjusting one's behaviour to others and forming positive relationships. Lack of social skills may lead to negative inter-actions with teaching and non-teaching staff and with other children. As a result a pupil may become socially isolated, rejected, labelled and stigmatised. They may resort to dis-ruptive or deviant behaviour in order to seek attention, gain acceptance or avoid humili-ation. Children lacking social skills may benefit from social skills training but they need to be motivated to do so, especially if they are otherwise achieving attention and accept-ance through disruption and deviance. Methods of teaching social skills include direct instruction, role-playing, game-playing skills and instruction in social skills strategies.

Barratt, P., Border, J., Joy, H., Parkinson, A. and Thomas G. (2000) *Developing Pupils' Social Communication Skills: Practical Resources*. London: David Fulton Publishers.
Warden, D. and Christie, D. (1997) *Teaching Social Behaviour: Classroom Activities to Foster Children's Interpersonal Awareness*. London: David Fulton Publishers.

Soft neurological signs

Some pupils with SpLD are said to manifest soft neurological signs of their learning difficulty. 'Soft' refers to signs that are fine, subtle and minor. Interpretation of these signs can be problematic. Soft neurological signs include clumsiness, hyperactivity, mild co-ordination difficulties, visual-motor deficiencies, language delay, confusing left with right and failure to establish a lateral preference. However, it should be noted that soft neuro-logical signs can occur in pupils who are learning satisfactorily and that there may be developmental lags before maturity is achieved. Tests for soft neurological signs are more psychological than neurological tests.

Special educational needs

The Education Act (1996), section 312, defines children as having special educational needs if they experience a learning difficulty that requires special educational provision.

Children have a learning difficulty if they have a greater difficulty in learning than most of the children of the same age, or if they have a disability that prevents or restricts them from using educational facilities used by children of the same age. A 'disability' is not necessarily a 'learning difficulty', as a child may experience a disability that does not prevent or restrict the use of educational facilities generally provided for children of the same age. A child may also have a difficulty in learning that is not a learning difficulty because the difficulty is not significantly greater than that of the majority of children of the same age. The learning difficulty has to be significant enough to be eligible for special educational provision, either within a mainstream school or, alternatively, in a special school. The SEN Code of Practice lays out the arrangements and criteria for statutory assessment, guidance on statements and special educational provision.

Specific learning disabilities (SpLD)

A pupil has a specific learning difficulty in a particular curricular area, such as reading or mathematics, but otherwise functions normally in other parts of the curriculum. Boys are identified more often with SpLD than girls. This may be due to biological or cultural factors or the pressure of expectations. There are different types of SpLD including dyslexia, dyscalculia, dysgraphia and dyspraxia. These different types of SpLD are not mutually exclusive and a pupil may have a combination of disabilities. There are different estimates of the prevalence of SpLD depending on definitions and criteria that are applied to pupil populations. Pupils having SpLD are of at least average intelligence and their disabilities cannot be attributed to sensory impairments, health problems, emotional and behavioural difficulties or inappropriate or inadequate teaching. SpLD pupils fail to make sufficient progress in reading, writing and mathematics and manifest a discrepancy between their measured intelligence and their educational achievement. The suggested causes of SpLD include genetic (family and twin studies) and neurological (brain dysfunction) factors, weaknesses in phonological awareness and rapid automatic naming and visual perceptual deficiencies.

Bender, W. (2001) *Learning Disabilities: Characteristics, Identification and Teaching Strategies* (4th edn). Boston, MA: Allyn & Bacon.

Lerner, J. (2003) *Learning Disabilities* (9th edn). Boston, MA: Houghton Mifflin.

Silver, A.A. and Hagin. R.A. (2002) *Disorders of Learning in Childhood* (2nd edn). New York: Wiley.

Swanson, H.L. (1999) *Interventions for Students with Learning Disabilities: Meta-Analysis of Treatment Outcomes*. New York: Guilford Press.

Swanson, H.L., Harris, K.R. and Graham, S. (2003) *Handbook of Learning Disabilities*. New York: Guilford Press.

Turkington, C. and Harris, J. (2002) *The Encyclopedia of Learning Disabilities*. New York: Facts on File.

Westwood, P. (2004) *Learning and Learning Difficulties*. London: David Fulton Publishers.

Speech disorders

Speech disorders are different from language disorders; they are abnormalities or deficiencies of speech and take the form of articulation difficulties (inability to pronounce a particular sound), problems with the voice (hoarseness) or difficulties with fluency (stammering or stuttering). Language disorders cover the whole spectrum of communication including delayed speech, disorders of vocabulary, meaning, comprehension, grammar and syntax.

Spelling difficulties

Spelling is difficult because in English the written form of the language has an inconsistent pattern. There is no one-to-one correspondence between the sounds of English and its written form. Spelling a word is more difficult than reading it due to the fact that there are several clues for reading a word, but spelling provides no such clues. Most children with learning difficulties experience spelling difficulties. The majority of poor spellers find it difficult to remember the correct sequence of letters. Spelling difficulties often continue after reading skills have been acquired. Spelling difficulties can have their origin in poor phonological awareness, poor visual strategies and inadequate or insufficient teaching. Those children with poor phonological awareness do not recognise phonemes within spoken words and will experience difficulties in the spelling and sound connections that are needed for spelling. Some children with poor visual strategies find it difficult to visualise the word or to store images of letters or the order of the letters in their visual memories. Other children have poor auditory memories and find it difficult to store sounds or syllables. Some children may be adversely affected by not being formally taught spelling and also by the lack of spelling practice. Strategies for improving spelling include phonemic awareness training, phonics teaching, visual-perceptual training in word and letter forms ('Look-Say-Cover-Write-Check' strategy), spelling practice using games, computer-assisted learning (use of a word processor), paired tutoring, the use of word families and multi-sensory methods.

Cryer, L. (2002) *SpellTrack Workbook: Spelling Activities for Key Stages 1 and 2*. London: David Fulton Publishers.

Walton, M (1998) *Teaching Reading and Spelling to Dyslexic Children*. London: David Fulton Publishers.

Westwood, P.S. (2004) *Spelling: Approaches to Teaching and Assessment*. London: David Fulton Publishers.

Stages in learning

Children proceed through a number of proficiency stages when learning new skills and knowledge. These include the attention or concentration stage, acquisition stage (acquiring skills), practice stage (practising skills), the fluency or automaticity stage (performing skills automatically), the maintenance stage (rehearsing and reviewing skills), the generalisation stage (applying skills in different or new contexts) and the adaptation stage (modifying skills to meet the demands of new contexts). Teachers need to provide relevant support at the different stages including direct teaching and pupil-centred activities, modelling skills, creating opportunities for practice, enabling pupils to rehearse and review skills and helping pupils to use their skills in new contexts.

Standardised tests

Standardised norm-referenced tests are used to evaluate a pupil's performance and achievement. One such test is the WISC-IV (Wechsler Intelligence Scale for Children, Fourth Edition). This test is an intelligence test. Standardised tests are judged on standardisation (On what population was the test standardised?), reliability (Are the results consistent through time?) and validity (Does the test measure what it claims to measure?). These tests form part of an assessment process but it is worth noting that they have limitations, that it is not wise to focus on one score and that it is necessary to include other sources in the assessment process. These tests may not provide sufficient information about the pupil; they may not assess the pupil in relation to the taught curriculum, they may induce teachers to teach to the test and they may focus on a narrow range of skills rather than on creativity.

Statement

A statement is a document describing a child's special educational needs and is drawn up by an LEA under the Education Act 1996, section 324. A statement is usually issued when it is decided by an LEA that a child's special educational needs cannot be met using the resources available to mainstream schools within that LEA. The issuing of a statement is preceded by presenting the parents with a draft copy, by setting out arrangements for parental choice of schools, the parents' right to make representations about the statement and the right to appeal to a Special Educational Needs and Disability Tribunal. The statement is reviewed at least once a year (Annual Review) in order to review progress towards the targets set out in the statement. The statement can be updated and the level of support or provision be adjusted if required. Sometimes, after an Annual Review, if sufficient progress has been achieved the LEA can withdraw the additional resources but will continue to monitor the child through a Monitoring Statement. After a Year 9 Annual Review, a Transition Plan is drawn up to support the pupil in their transition from school to adult life. Most children with statements are educated in mainstream schools. A child receiving a statement will usually have an IEP (Individual Education Plan) setting out the extra support and strategies being provided along with specific targets and review dates.

Statutory assessment

A detailed assessment of a child's special educational needs (SEN) in order to identify their needs and the provision required to meet those needs. As well as a parent, other people such as a GP can refer a child to the LEA. The assessment process includes information and advice from teaching staff, advice from an educational psychologist and from other relevant professionals. After the advice has been collected and collated it is discussed by the Special Educational Needs Panel. This panel decides whether the child receives a statement of special educational needs. The LEA may decide that the needs can be met within the school or early years setting. If this is the case, a 'note in lieu' can be issued explaining why a statement has not been made and what the school can provide to meet the child's needs.

Stereotyped behaviour

Persistent, repetitive actions that appear purposeless or non-functional. These actions are rigid and inflexible and do not change according to context. This type of behaviour can be manifested by children with severe learning difficulties and includes rocking, hand flapping, head banging and hair pulling. Children may engage in stereotyped behaviour, or stereotypy as a form of self-regulation serves to control levels of stimulation. Children may maintain these behaviours because they evoke pleasurable feelings or because they isolate or insulate them from what they perceive as threatening environments.

Strategy training

This involves teaching pupils action plans that they can use when approaching and attempting learning tasks. Strategy training for pupils with learning difficulties includes strategies to improve writing skills. These strategies focus on organising thoughts (brainstorming), on planning (writing drafts) and on revision (proofreading). They are based on a step-by-step or staged approach to learning that requires pupil self-talk or self-instruction. Teachers can teach these strategies through direct teaching, modelling and guided practice.

Subtypes

Subtypes are subgroups or additional different types of a general category such as dyslexia and dyscalculia. Subtypes of dyslexia include visual and auditory dyslexia, dyseidetic and dysphonetic dyslexia, logographic dyslexia and alphabetic dyslexia, phonological dyslexia and surface dyslexia. It is unclear how far these subtypes are distinct from one another, how far they overlap and how far they are useful for designing appropriate teaching programmes to address the specifics of such subtypes.

Syndrome

A syndrome is a group of symptoms that appear to occur regularly together in a pattern that can be identified or classified with a special or particular term. In psychology, psychiatry and medicine it is a cluster or group of symptoms that can occur together and that are believed to be indicative of a particular abnormality, deficiency or medical condition, e.g. Asperger syndrome, Down's syndrome and Fragile X syndrome. Every symptom or aspect of a syndrome is not necessarily present in any one individual.

Synthetic phonics

A skills-based approach to the teaching of reading. It begins with sounds and letters and then moves on to word building and decoding. It depends on the learner having good auditory discrimination, good sound blending skills and the capacity to store and recall sound–symbol correspondences from long-term memory.

Targets

Targets can be skills- or knowledge-based, that is learning a specific skill or acquiring knowledge by a particular time or over a particular period. It is often suggested that targets should be SMART, that is specific, measurable, achievable, relevant and time-related. Target setting is based on the outcomes of an assessment process. It is recommended that the number of targets should be limited to three or four and that after a period of time progress towards those targets should be reviewed. The review should be guided by success criteria, by criteria measuring or determining whether the targets have been achieved, partially achieved or not achieved at all. After a review or reassessment the targets may be changed or modified and the interventions or strategies used also changed or modified.

Task analysis

The aim of task analysis is to plan sequential steps for learning a specific skill. It breaks down or divides up a task into easier steps or stages. The steps of task analysis include stating the learning task, breaking the task into steps and placing them in a sequence, determining what steps can already be performed and then teaching in sequence each step.

Teacher expectancy

Teachers' perceptions of the causes or factors underlying learning difficulties are varied. However, there is a tendency among teachers to see the main causes of learning difficulties as being due to within-child factors (child-deficit model) or home background. Within-child deficits cited by teachers include biological and neurological deficits, delays in maturation, sensory impairments and attitudinal or motivational problems. The problem with a child-deficit and home background explanation is that it can lead teachers to be pessimistic about teaching children with learning difficulties effectively. Teachers may therefore have low expectations of children's progress or success. Although within-child factors may contribute to a child's learning difficulties, inadequate teaching can also contribute to a child's problems.

Teaching methods

Teaching methods used with children with learning difficulties include activity and exploratory-based, behavioural, direct and explicit methods.

Tests and testing

There are formal and informal tests. Formal tests include diagnostic tests used to assess children's knowledge and their repertoire of skills. They also identify children's strengths and weaknesses in particular areas. Diagnostic reading tests include tests of phonic knowledge, of phonemic awareness, of decoding skills and of word recognition. Language tests include comprehension tests, tests of syntax and written language. There are also tests for visual and auditory acuity. Other tests exist to assess visual-motor, gross and fine motor skills. With respect to mathematics there are formal tests such as standardised and group surveys (tests giving an overall achievement level) and diagnostic mathematics tests and individual achievement tests. There are also informal tests that test pupils on the materials used in classroom. The advantage of these tests is that they are close to the actual learning process and they give teachers freedom to devise tests to suit their objectives. They can also be given frequently and over an extended period of time during lesson time. With regard to reading, children can be tested while they are reading aloud. Teachers can assess the child's general reading level, word-recognition ability, types of error and comprehension of texts. Informal reading inventories (IRIs) are useful for assessing a child's reading levels. Some IRIs are published; others can be constructed by teachers. There is also miscue analysis to assess oral reading. Miscues are mistakes or errors made while reading orally.

Kamin, L.J. (1974) *The Science and Politics of IQ*. New York: Wiley.

Lerner, J. (2003) *Learning Disabilities* (9th edn). Boston, MA: Houghton Mifflin.

Murphy, K.R. and Davidshofer, C.O. (1998) *Psychological Testing: Principles and Applications* (4th edn). Upper Saddle River, NJ: Prentice-Hall.

Rust, J. and Golombok, S. (1999) *Modern Psychometrics* (2nd edn). London: Routledge.

Westwood, P. (2004) *Numeracy and Learning Difficulties: Approaches to Teaching and Assessment*. London: David Fulton Publishers.

Westwood, P. (2004) *Reading and Learning Difficulties: Approaches to Teaching and Assessment*. London: David Fulton Publishers.

Text-processing problems

Poor readers frequently experience text-processing difficulties. They are over-dependent on using context to learn unfamiliar words because of problems with orthographic or phonological processing. The lack of automaticity and fluency means that less attention is focused on comprehending text. Furthermore, poor readers often remain at the basic level of comprehension, failing to move on to higher levels of comprehension such as reflecting, inferring, predicting and questioning. Children with comprehension difficulties can be taught comprehension strategies. These strategies include monitoring comprehension – that is the developing awareness of their comprehension processes – collaborative learning through engaging peer support, the use of graphic and semantic organisers to represent texts, answering and asking questions about texts, using knowledge of text structure to answer questions about texts, and summarising – that is generalising from texts. Before, during and after reading, teachers can implement various strategies that facilitate the comprehension of texts. These strategies are based on building background knowledge, predicting text, questioning text, using graphic organisers, engaging in self-monitoring, identifying difficulties and solutions and summarising.

Theories of learning

Theories of learning include behavioural, cognitive-behavioural, social learning and constructivist. Behavioural theory is based on behaviourist principles, as in classical and operant conditioning. Cognitive theory is based on information processing. Social learning theory is based on observational learning and modelling. Constructivist theory is based on active participation in the social construction of learning. These theories have different implications for children with learning difficulties. Behaviour theory encourages the use of functional analysis that includes formal observation, target setting, prompting responses, shaping responses and positive reinforcement. Cognitive theory encourages the use of self-management, self-monitoring and self-evaluation. Social learning theory encourages observational learning, modelling, self-efficacy and self-regulation. Constructivist theory encourages self-reflection, collaborative and exploratory learning, and scaffolding.

Westwood, P. (2004) *Learning and Learning Difficulties*. London: David Fulton Publishers.

Time management

This is important in addressing the problems presented by children with short attention spans. Learning tasks should be short, manageable, varied and interspersed with appropriate breaks. Pupils can use charts, lists and diagrams to develop a sense of time and also what they can achieve in allotted time spans.

Transition plan

A transition plan is a plan drawn up after the Year 9 Annual Review of a statement and is intended to help plan the transition to adult life of a child with SEN. Any later annual reviews should include a transition plan. At these annual reviews information should be sought from social services in order to determine whether the child is disabled and whether the local authority will be required to provide support when the child leaves school. Other external agencies should also be consulted such as the educational psychology service. Information concerning the transition plan is laid out in the SEN Code of Practice (DfES 2001).

Truancy

Unauthorised absence from school. It increases particularly after Year 10 when GCSE courses begin. Many truants engage in post-registration truancy, absenting themselves from school or lessons after registration. Truants frequently report that they dislike a particular teacher or lesson or experience subjects as irrelevant or uninteresting. Children who truant from school include children with learning difficulties, for example those who are poor readers. These truants may experience the National Curriculum and associated learning tasks as difficult and irrelevant. They may also experience failure, stigma and humiliation in particular lessons or in school generally. These experiences may contribute to truancy from certain lessons or from school. Absence from school or lessons compounds learning difficulties and leads to increasing truancy and a vicious circle of truancy and educational failure. Children fall further behind and find it difficult to catch up on missed work. Unless the learning difficulties are successfully addressed the likelihood of truancy increases.

Underachievement

A discrepancy between a child's ability and their actual educational achievement. The child's actual achievement, as reflected in tests and examination results, does not reflect their actual ability and potential. The child fails to achieve their potential due to factors other than ability. These other factors might be internal or external to the child, for example emotional problems or inadequate teaching. With reference to different types of specific learning disabilities the discrepancy is between measured ability (usually by an IQ test) and achievement in terms of reading, writing, spelling and mathematics.

VAKT (Visual, Auditory, Kinaesthetic and Tactile Learning)

A multi-sensory approach to teaching reading that uses all senses to improve reading achievement. Pupils hear the teacher pronounce the word, they say the word to themselves, they hear the word and feel the movement and the surface as they trace the word. There are several multi-sensory methods including the Orton-Gillingham Method, the Wilson Reading System and the Fernald Method.

Vision impairment

Vision impairment can be associated with learning difficulties. A child having difficulty with visual and spatial processing is likely to experience problems with learning. Visual impairment is a term that refers to any eye condition that is not improved by spectacles. Children with impaired vision (blindness) are unable to learn through imitation and observation, and even partially sighted children have to make a disproportionate effort and allow more time to process information through the use of various aids. Particular visual impairment difficulties include delays in motor skill development, the effective use of partial sight and the development of concepts. A particular child's visual impairment can be affected by a number of factors such as the type of visual defect, the age it appears, prior learning experiences, access to learning aids and motivation.

Arter, C., Mason, H., McCall, S., McLindin, M. and Stone, J. (1999) *Children with Visual Impairment in Mainstream Settings*. London: David Fulton Publishers.
Mason, H. and McCall, S. (eds) (1997) *Visual Impairment*. London: David Fulton Publishers.

Visual acuity

The ability to see letters from a specified distance. The Snellen chart is frequently used. It tests visual acuity at 20 feet from the chart, far-point acuity. Other devices are needed to assess near-point visual acuity at 16 inches, the distance at which reading occurs. Refractive errors are caused by a defect in the lens. There are three kinds: myopia (near-sightedness), hyperopia (far-sightedness) and astigmatism (blurring). However, difficulties with binocular vision can have more important implications for reading. This occurs when the two eyes are not working together. Binocular difficulties include strabismus (lack of co-ordination), inadequate fusion (lack of fusion of the two images) and aniseikonia (unequal size or shape of two images). However, reading is probably more affected by problems with visual discrimination and perception than visual acuity.

Visual discrimination

The ability to distinguish one object from another one. With regard to reading ability visual discrimination refers to discriminating or distinguishing between letters and words.

Visual imaging

The ability to visualise and store images of letters and words in visual memory. Even when it is the case that children have achieved the phonetic stage of spelling competence, they may appear unable to progress further if they do not use visual strategies to store images of words in their visual memories. It is suggested that children should have training in visual imaging of letters and words to promote spelling development, an example being 'Look-Say-Cover-Write-Check'.

Visual perceptual and motor difficulties

Children with mathematical disabilities may experience problems with tasks that involve visual motor and visual perception abilities. Some children may experience problems in seeing number symbols, in counting by pointing; others find it difficult to see objects in sets or to see and identify geometrical shapes. These children may also experience difficulties in copying geometrical shapes and numbers. Their handwriting may also be poor, leading to inaccuracy in writing down and aligning numbers.

Vocabulary

Children with learning difficulties often have limited and restricted vocabularies. In order to read effectively it is necessary to build up an extensive vocabulary. Knowledge of vocabulary is closely connected to reading achievement. A restricted vocabulary limits comprehension and concept development. Vocabulary can be expanded in various ways such as through highlighting multiple meanings of words, e.g. 'note'. This highlighting can occur through the use of dictionary games and sentence-completion exercises. Other ways include finding new sources of vocabulary and new words from magazines, television and advertising. Vocabulary can also be increased through vertical and horizontal classification, that is breaking down a word such as 'rabbit' into subcategories or differentiating a word such as 'cat' so that it is not used to apply to all animals. Word webs can also be used to expand vocabulary by developing word associations. The cloze procedure can also be used to increase vocabulary by deleting only newly learned words.

Wechsler Intelligence Scale for Children (WISC)

The WISC is an intelligence or IQ test developed in 1949 to measure the intelligence of children ages 5 to 15 years. There have been a number of revisions. There is also a pre-school version – the Wechsler Preschool and Primary Stage of Intelligence (WPPSI) – and an adult version – the Wechsler Adult Intelligence Scale (WAIS). This test is made up of 13 subtests organised into two groups, that is Verbal and Performance Scales. It provides three IQ scores: verbal, performance and full-scale IQ. The WISC provides verbal, performance and full-scale deviation IQs based on a mean of 100 and a standard deviation of 15. The WISC has high reliability and predictive validity. Information collected through the test includes information about a child's strengths and weaknesses in language and performance. This information is arrived at through comparing the verbal score to the Performance score. One of the main uses of the WISC in special education is to compare a child's ability with their level of achievement in order to identify a specific learning disability. There are various methods and formulae for calculating ability–achievement discrepancies and there are also limitations to ability–achievement discrepancy analysis. These limitations include age range limits and limited exposure to learning experience. Furthermore, severe discrepancy does not necessarily indicate a learning disability. Other evidence is needed to support a diagnosis of a specific learning disability. The disability must not be due to factors such as visual or hearing impairment, mental disability, medical conditions, emotional or behavioural difficulties and educational or socio-economic deprivation. There are controversies regarding the measurement of intelligence and the use of IQ tests. These controversies involve issues concerning bias in test measurement, bias in prediction, test fairness, cultural bias, the heritability of intelligence and the consistency and modifiability of IQ.

Whole language approach

One of two main approaches to reading, the other being a 'skills-based approach'. The whole language or 'meaning-emphasis' approach is described as a holistic approach to reading and refers to obtaining the meaning of words and sentences through the use of context and syntax rather than through phonic decoding. This approach includes methods such as 'guided reading', 'shared book experience', 'language-experience approach' and 'literature-based reading'. This approach stresses authentic and natural learning situations and purposeful reading. Children are encouraged to immerse themselves in language-rich, real books and to reflect and discuss texts they read in a purposeful way. They are also encouraged to write up drafts, edit and revise their stories with feedback from other children and their teachers. Teachers intervene when required, and when specific skills need to be taught they are taught within the reading or writing context. The stated advantages of this approach are that it helps children during the early stages of learning, that it helps to develop purposive reading, that it motivates children to read books and to write, that it develops interpretative strategies and that it increases vocabulary. However, it may not be appropriate for all children as the absence of direct instruction and structured learning may not suit children with learning difficulties or who are socially and economically disadvantaged. This approach has been criticised for undervaluing direct instruction in the alphabetic principle and the teaching of decoding skills. It has also been criticised for not understanding that the use of contextual cues and real books can be difficult for reading beginners and older children with reading difficulties. There is an ongoing controversy over the whole language and the skills-based approaches. However, it is probably the case that teachers use a combination of both approaches. There is a debate over a balanced approach incorporating elements of both whole language and skills-based approaches. The balance of elements includes a combination of direct instruction with child-centred learning tailored to individual needs and individual learning tasks. At certain stages or times the balance of elements may need to change in order to meet changing needs. Literacy development requires that word recognition skills are acquired, that children engage in intensive reading practice, that children read independently at an appropriate level, that they use appropriate reading strategies and that they experience pleasure in reading.

Chall, J. (1967) *Learning to Read: The Great Debate*. New York: McGraw-Hill.

Pressley, M. (1998) *Reading Instruction that Works: The Case for Balanced Teaching*. New York: Guilford Press.

Tilstone, C., Lacey, P., Porter, J. and Robertson, C. (2000) *Pupils with Learning Difficulties in Mainstream Schools*. London: David Fulton Publishers.

Westwood, P. (2004) *Reading and Learning Difficulties*. London: David Fulton Publishers.

Withdrawal model of support

The withdrawal model is one where children with learning difficulties are withdrawn from mainstream classrooms to receive intensive one-to-one or small group support. A number of criticisms have been made of the withdrawal model. These include that pupils receive fragmented and disrupted learning experiences; that there is deskilling of mainstream teachers and that mainstream teachers are absolved from their responsibilities; that pupils are stigmatised; and that it is ineffective in raising achievement. The emphasis now is on in-class support along with a whole-school approach. However, it can be the case that in the mainstream classroom the child experiences undifferentiated work; the lack or even absence of intensive, individualised support from the class or subject teacher; and may even feel stigmatised.

Word blindness

Word blindness or alexia is a disability characterised by the partial or total loss of the ability to identify the written word. There is no visual impairment and no inability to identify the spoken word.

Word processing

Word processing is an effective means of teaching writing. It facilitates writing for children with learning difficulties. Pupils can write without being overly concerned about handwriting and can redraft without making a mess of writing. Word processing can help to motivate pupils enabling them to produce neat, error-free text. It can also facilitate collaboration between teacher and pupils and pupils and their peers. Revision, reviewing, redrafting and correcting of text is made easier and it can also help to improve fine motor skills.

Word recognition

The ability to read requires learners to recognise words. After children have developed word recognition they can concentrate on reading for meaning. Without the skills of word recognition children are unable to proceed to higher-level cognitive skills. The learner who concentrates excessively on word recognition will have little capacity for comprehension. Early achievement of word recognition is necessary because it predicts ability in reading comprehension. Learners need to recognise words easily, quickly and automatically. Word recognition skills include phonics (synthetic and analytic phonics), recognition of sight words, context cues (recognition of words through the context of the word) and structural analysis (recognition of words through analysis of units such as syllables, prefixes (word beginnings), suffixes (word endings), compound and root words). Pupils should be taught to use all the word recognition skills but in general they will only use them when they come across unfamiliar words. Pupils will require direct instruction in these skills. Some will need phonological awareness training and some will require intensive practice in developing sight vocabularies. Many children will need to be taught phonics and structural analysis strategies in order to decode and spell proficiently.

Working memory

Short-term memory. This type of memory processes the current visual and verbal information that an individual is focusing on for a particular reason. The information is then stored temporarily. Working memory is essential for reading comprehension and verbal communication. Children with learning difficulties experience problems with remembering information. Strategies for addressing these problems include rehearsal (repeating the information), grouping (putting information into categories), organising (relating parts of the information) and key words (linking unfamiliar to familiar words).

Writing difficulties

Writing is a complex process that requires learners to form and organise ideas in a logical sequence, choose appropriate vocabulary and syntax, punctuate and spell correctly. The learner needs to integrate various functions such as attention and language, long- and short-term memory with specific skills such as motor skills. With regard to texts, learners need to be able to edit, review and evaluate what they have written as well as to address particular audiences. Children generally proceed through a number of writing stages such as the pre-phonetic stage and the phonetic stage until they reach a stage where they use various writing strategies that enable them to achieve independence. Children with learning difficulties experience particular problems with metacognitive skills such as self-regulation and self-monitoring required for transcription. These children may also experience deficits in working memory. They often have weaknesses in the areas of forming and organising ideas, editing, reviewing and revising text and also in terms of strategies for addressing their writing difficulties. In order to address a child's writing difficulties teachers need to assess the child through direct observation, by sampling work and by testing specific skills. Assessment should focus on the various aspects of writing including spelling, punctuation, grammar, content and level of complexity. Curriculum-based assessment is recommended as this type of assessment gets closer to the child's writing context. Teachers can ameliorate writing difficulties through modifying the task and by using a variety of approaches such as direct instruction, precision teaching, guided practice and modelling. The child can be taught specific writing strategies that enable the child to form and organise ideas for writing. Children are helped by the use of planning sheets and graphic organisers that provide frameworks for their writing. Other strategies include written conversations, personal diaries, patterned writing and drawing pictures. Pre-writing strategies such as brainstorming, editing strategies such as checking text for clarity and accuracy, and post-writing strategies such as proofreading are also helpful. The use of a word processor can help teachers display to children the whole process of writing and also assist children in transcribing their ideas into writing. Word processing can help to motivate children, facilitate collaboration between teachers, children and their peers, facilitate drafting, editing and revising and even help with fine motor skills. Word processors also have specialised functions such as spell and grammar checkers that can help to facilitate writing.

Chapman, C. and King, R. (2003) *Differentiated Instructional Strategies for Writing in the Content Areas*. Thousand Oaks, CA: Corwin Press.

Edwards, S.A. (2003) *Ways of Writing with Young Kids*. Boston, MA: Allyn & Bacon.

Lewin, L. (2003) *Paving the Way in Reading and Writing*. San Francisco, CA: Jossey-Bass.

Olson, C.B. (2003) *The Reading/Writing Connection: Strategies for Teaching and Learning in the Secondary Classroom*. Boston, MA: Allyn & Bacon.

Z

Zone of proximal development

A concept introduced and developed by Vygotsky. It is defined as the learning that can easily be achieved with the support and guidance of a teacher. It is the gap between what a pupil has achieved and what they could achieve with the support of a teacher or peer. It provides a foundation on which teachers can build and develop their pupils' learning. It also connects with the idea of readiness or preparedness and the idea of scaffolding. There are a number of levels, the lower level being independence, where the pupil can learn on their own, and the upper level where the pupil finds it impossible to acquire new knowledge and skills even with the support of a teacher or their peers. Learning that is within the pupil's zone of potentiality has a high degree of success but learning beyond that zone may end up in failure. Progress in learning within this zone is dependent on co-operative and collaborative group work and discussion within the groups. Pupils, by collaborating and co-operating in groups, are in a stronger position to address challenging learning tasks and become independent learners.

Daniels, H. (2001) *Vygotsky and Pedagogy*. London: Routledge-Falmer.
Vygotsky, L.S. (1962) *Thought and Language*. Cambridge, MA: MIT Press.

Bibliography

Adams, M.J., Foorman, B.R., Lundberg, I. and Beeler, T. (1998) *Phonemic Awareness in Young Children: A Classroom Curriculum*. Baltimore, MD: Brookes.

Aird, R. (2001) *The Education and Care of Children with Severe Profound and Multiple Learning Difficulties*. London: David Fulton Publishers.

Alban-Metcalfe, J. and Alban-Metcalfe, J. (2001) *Managing Attention Deficit-Hyperactivity Disorder in the Inclusive Classroom*. London: David Fulton Publishers.

APA (1994) *Diagnostic and Statistical Manual of Mental Disorders* (4th edn). Washington, DC: American Psychological Association.

Arter, C., Mason, H., McCall, S., McLinden, M. and Stone, J. (1999) *Children with Visual Impairment in Mainstream Settings*. London: David Fulton Publishers.

Ayers, H., Clarke, D. and Murray, A. (2000) *Perspectives on Behaviour* (2nd edn). London: David Fulton Publishers.

Ayers, H. and Prytys, C. (2002) *An A to Z Practical Guide to Emotional and Behavioural Difficulties*. London: David Fulton Publishers.

Bandura, A. (1977) *Social Learning Theory*. Morristown, NJ: General Learning.

Bandura, A. (1997) *Self-Efficacy: The Exercise of Control*. New York: Freeman.

Banich, M.T. (1997) *Neuropsychology: The Neural Bases of Mental Function*. Boston, MA: Houghton Mifflin.

Barriga, N.C. and Erin, J.N. (2001) *Visual Impairment and Learning* (4th edn). Austin, TX: ProEd.

Barrow, G., Bradshaw, E. and Newton, T. (2001) *Improving Behaviour and Raising Self-Esteem in the Classroom: A Practical Guide to Using Transactional Analysis*. London: David Fulton Publishers.

Beaumont, J.G., Kenealy, P.M. and Rogers, M.J.C. (eds) (1996) *The Blackwell Dictionary of Neuropsychology*. Oxford: Blackwell.

Bender, W. (2001) *Learning Disabilities: Characteristics, Identification and Teaching Strategies* (4th edn). Boston, MA: Allyn and Bacon.

Berger, A. and Gross, J. (eds) (1999) *Teaching the Literacy Hour in an Inclusive Classroom*. London: David Fulton Publishers.

Berger, A., Buck, D. and Davis, V. (eds) (2001) *Assessing Pupils' Performance Using the P Levels*. London: David Fulton Publishers.

Berger, A. and Morris, D. (2001) *Implementing the Literacy Hour for Pupils with Learning Difficulties* (2nd edn). London: David Fulton Publishers.

Blair-Larsen, S.M. and Williams, K.A. (eds) (1990) *The Balanced Reading Programme.* Newark, DE: International Reading Association.

Bley, N.S. and Thornton, C.A. (1995) *Teaching Mathematics to Students with Learning Disabilities* (3rd edn). Austin, TX: ProEd.

Booker, G., Bond, D., Briggs, J. and Davey, G. (1997) *Teaching Primary Mathematics* (2nd edn). Melbourne: Addison-Wesley Longman.

Bradley, R., Danielson, L. and Hallahan, D.P. (eds) (2002) *Identification of Learning Disabilities: Research to Practice.* Mahwah, NJ: Erlbaum.

Bristow, J., Crowley, P. and Daines, B. (1999) *Memory and Learning: A Practical Guide for Teachers.* London: David Fulton Publishers.

Brophy, J.E. (2001) *Motivating Students to Learn.* Boston, MA: McGraw-Hill.

Browne, A. (1998) *A Practical Guide in Teaching in the Early Years.* London: Chapman.

Bruner, J.S. (1996) *Towards a Theory of Instruction.* Cambridge, MA: Harvard University Press.

Burnett, A. and Wylie, J. (2002) *Soundaround: Developing Phonological Awareness Skills in the Foundation Stage.* London: David Fulton Publishers.

Carr, A. (1999) *The Handbook of Child and Adolescent Clinical Psychology: A Contextual Approach.* London: Routledge.

Carver, R.P. (2000) *The Causes of High and Low Reading Achievement.* Mahwah, NJ: Erlbaum.

Ceci, S.J. (1996) *On Intelligence* (2nd edn). Cambridge, MA: Harvard University Press.

Cheminais, R. (2003) *Closing the Inclusion Gap: Special and Mainstream Schools Working in Partnership.* London: David Fulton Publishers.

Clay, M.M. (1985) *The Early Detection of Reading Difficulties.* Auckland, NZ: Heinemann.

Clay, M.M. (1994) *A Guidebook for Reading Recovery Teachers.* Porstmouth, NH: Heinemann.

Cole, P. and Chan, L. (1990) *Methods and Strategies for Special Education.* New York: Prentice-Hall.

Collins, M. and Cheek, E.H. (1984) *Diagnostic-Prescriptive Reading Instruction: A Guide for Classroom Teachers* (2nd edn). Dubuque, IA: Brown.

Cooper, C. (1999) *Intelligence and Abilities.* London: Routledge.

Cooper, P. and Bilton. K.M. (2002) *Attention Deficit/Hyperactivity Disorder: A Practical Guide for Teachers* (2nd edn). London: David Fulton Publishers.

Cooper, P. *et al.* (1994) *Emotional and Behavioural Difficulties.* London: Routledge.

Cowne, E. (2003) *The SENCO Handbook: Working Within a Whole-School Approach* (4th edn). London: David Fulton Publishers.

Creemers, B. (1994) *The Effective Classroom.* London: Cassell.

Cullingford, C. (2001) *How Children Learn to Read and How to Help Them.* London: Kogan Page.

Cumine, V., Leach, J. and Stevenson, G. (1998) *Asperger Syndrome: A Practical Guide for Teachers.* London: David Fulton Publishers.

Cumine, V., Leach, J. and Stevenson, G. (2000) *Autism in the Early Years: A Practical Guide*. London: David Fulton Publishers.

Cunningham, P. (2000) *Phonics They Use: Words for Reading and Writing* (3rd edn). New York: Longmans.

Daniels, H. (2001) *Vygotsky and Pedagogy*. London: Routledge-Falmer.

Deary, I.J. (2001) *Intelligence: A Very Short Introduction*. Oxford: Oxford University Press.

Dockrell, J. and McShane, J. (1992) *Children's Learning Difficulties: A Cognitive Approach*. Oxford: Blackwell.

Donlan, C. (ed.) (1998) *The Development of Mathematical Skills*. Hove: Erlbaum.

Drifte, C. (2003) *Handbook for Pre-School SEN Provision: The Code of Practice in Relation to the Early Years* (2nd edn). London: David Fulton Publishers.

Emerson, E. (1995) *Challenging Behaviour: Analysis and Intervention in People with Learning Difficulties*. Cambridge: Cambridge University Press.

Emler, N. (2001) *Self-esteem: The Costs and Causes of Low Self-worth*. York: Joseph Rowntree Foundation York Publishing Services.

Epanchin, B.C. and Paul, J.L. (eds) (1987) *Emotional Problems of Childhood and Adolescence: A Multidisciplinary Perspective*. New York: Merrill.

Farrell, M. (2003) *The Special Education Handbook* (3rd edn). London: David Fulton Publishers.

Farrell, P. (1997) *Teaching Pupils with Learning Difficulties: Strategies and Solutions*. London: Cassell.

Fields, M. and Spangler, K.L. (2000) *Let's Begin Reading Right* (4th edn). Upper Saddle River, NJ: Merrill.

Fisher, B. and Medvic, E.F. (2000) *Perspectives in Shared Reading, Planning and Practice*. Porstmouth, NH: Heinemann.

Fiske, S.T. and Taylor, S.E. (1991) *Social Cognition*. New York. McGraw Hill, Inc.

Fountas, I.C. and Pinnell, G.S. (1999) *Matching Books to Readers* (2nd edn). Portsmouth, NH: Heinemann.

Frederickson, N. and Cline, T. (2002) *Special Educational Needs: Inclusion and Diversity*. Buckingham: Open University Press.

Galloway, D., Rogers, C., Armstrong, D. and Leo, E. (1998) *Motivating the Difficult to Teach*. London: Longman.

Gillet, J. and Temple, C. (2000) *Understanding Reading Problems: Assessment and Instruction* (5th edn). New York: Longman.

Glynn, T., McNaughton, S., Robinson, V. and Quinn, M. (1979) *Remedial Reading at Home*. Wellington: New Zealand Council for Educational Research.

Gorman, J.C. (2001) *Emotional Disorders and Learning Disabilities: Interactions and Interventions*. Thousand Oaks, CA: Corwin Press.

Gregory, G. and Chapman, C. (2002) *Differentiated Instructional Strategies: One Size Does Not Fit All*. Thousand Oaks, CA: Corwin Press.

Hall, D., Griffiths, D., Haslam, L. and Wilkin, Y. (2001) *Assessing the Needs of Bilingual Pupils: Living in Two Languages* (2nd edn). London: David Fulton Publishers.

Henderson, A. (1998) *Maths for the Dyslexic: A Practical Guide*. London: David Fulton Publishers.

Henley, M., Ramsey, R.S. and Algozzine, R. (2002) *Characteristics of and Strategies for Teaching Students with Mild Disabilities* (4th edn). Boston: Allyn & Bacon.

Herbert, M. (1998) *Clinical Child Psychology: Social Learning, Development and Behaviour* (2nd edn). Chichester: Wiley.

Hoien, T. and Lundberg, I. (2000) *Dyslexia: From Theory to Intervention.* Dordrecht: Kluwer.

Holdaway, D. (1982) 'Shared book experience: teaching reading using favourite books'. *Theory into Practice*, **21** (4); 293–300.

Holdaway, D. (1990) *Independence in Reading* (3rd edn). Sydney: Ashton Scholastic.

Howlin, P. (1998) *Children with Autism and Asperger Syndrome: A Guide for Practitioners and Carers.* Chichester: Wiley.

Johnson, M. and Parkinson, G. (2002) *Epilepsy: A Practical Guide.* London: David Fulton Publishers.

Jones, C.J. (1998) *Curriculum-Based Assessment the Easy Way.* Springfield IL: Charles C. Thomas.

Jordan, R. (1999) *Autistic Spectrum Disorder: An Introductory Handbook for Practitioners.* London: David Fulton Publishers.

Kamin, L.J. (1977) *The Science and Politics of IQ.* London: Penguin.

Kavale, K. (2002) 'Discrepancy models in the identification of learning disability', in R. Bradley, L. Danielson and D.P. Hallahan (eds) *Identification of Learning Disabilities: Research in Practice* Mahwah, NJ: Erlbaum, pp. 369–426.

Kirby, A. and Drew, S. (2002) *Guide to Dyspraxia and Developmental Coordination Disorders.* London: David Fulton Publishers.

Larcombe, A. (1985) *Mathematical Learning Difficulties in Secondary School.* Milton Keynes: Open University Press.

Leach, D.J. and Raybould, E.C. (1977) *Learning and Behaviour Difficulties in School.* London: Open Books.

Lerner, J. (2003) *Learning Disabilities: Theories, Diagnosis and Teaching* (9th edn). Boston, MA: Houghton Mifflin.

Leslie, L. (1997) *Authentic Literacy Assessment: An Ecological Approach.* New York: Longman.

Lindsley, O. (1992) 'Precision teaching: discoveries and effects'. *Journal of Applied Behaviour Analysis*, **25**(1); 51–7.

Lorenz, S. (1998) *Children with Down's Syndrome: A Guide for Teachers and Support Assistants in Mainstream Schools.* London: David Fulton Publishers.

McGuiness, D. (1998) *Why Children Can't Read.* London: Penguin.

Marlotti, A.S. and Homan, S.P. (2001) *Linking Reading Assessment to Instruction* (3rd edn). Mahwah, NJ: Erlbaum.

Marlowe, B.A. (1998) *Creating and Sustaining the Constructivist Classroom.* Thousand Oaks, CA: Corwin Press.

Marschark, M., Laing, H.G. and Alvertinini, J.A. (2002) *Educating Deaf Students: From Research to Practice.* Oxford: Oxford University Press.

Martin, D. and Miller, C. (2002) *Speech and Language Difficulties in the Classroom* (2nd edn). London: David Fulton Publishers.

Marvin, C. and Stokoe, C. (2003) *Access to Science: Curriculum Planning and Practical Activities for Pupils with Learning Difficulties.* London: David Fulton Publishers.

Mason, H. and McCall, S. (1997) *Visual Impairment: Access to Education for Children and Young People*. London: David Fulton Publishers.

Mercer, C.D. and Mercer, A.R. (1993) *Teaching Students with Learning Problems* (4th edn). New York: Merrill.

Mesibov, G. and Howley, M. (2003) *Assessing the Curriculum for Pupils with Autistic Spectrum Disorders: Using the TEACCH Programme to Help Inclusion*. London: David Fulton Publishers.

Miles, T.R. and Miles, E. (1992) *Dyslexia and Mathematics*. London: Routledge.

Miller, W.H. (1995) *Alternative Assessment Techniques for Reading and Writing*. West Nyack, NY: Centre for Applied Research in Education.

Minskoff, E. and Allsopp, D. (2003) *Academic Success Strategies for Adolescents with Learning Disabilities and ADHD*. Baltimore, MD: Brookes.

Mittler, P. (2000) *Working Towards Inclusive Education*. London: David Fulton Publishers.

Montgomery, D. (1990) *Children with Learning Difficulites*. London: Cassell.

Morton, J. (2004) *Understanding Developmental Disorders: A Causal Modelling Approach*. Oxford: Blackwell.

Murphy, K.R. and Davidshofer, C.O. (1998) *Psychological Testing: Principles and Applications* (4th edn). Upper Saddle River, NJ: Prentice-Hall.

National Reading Panel (US) (2000) *Teaching Children to Read: An Evidence-Based Assessment of the Scientific Research Literature on Reading and its Implication for Reading Instruction*. Washington, DC: National Institute of Child Health and Human Development. (http://www.nichd.nih.gov/publications/pubslist.cfm#RR)

Neale, M.D. (1999) *Neale Analysis of Reading Ability: Manual* (3rd edn). Melbourne: Australian Council for Educational Research.

Norwich, B. (1990) *Reappraising Special Needs Education*. London: Cassell.

O'Brien, T. (1998) *Promoting Positive Behaviour*. London: David Fulton Publishers.

O'Brien, T. and Guiney, D. (2001) *Differentiation in Teaching and Learning: Principles and Practice*. London: Continuum.

OECD (Organisation for Economic Co-operation and Development) (1999) *Inclusive Education at Work: Students with Disabilities in Mainstream Schools*. Paris: OECD Centre for Educational Research and Innovation.

Palinscar, A.S. and Brown, A.L. (1984) 'Reciprocal teaching of comprehension – fostering and monitoring activities'. *Cognition and Instruction*, **1**; 117–75.

Plomin, R. *et.al.* (1997) *Behavioral Genetics* (3rd edn). New York: W.H. Freeman and Company.

Pressley, M. (1998) *Reading Instruction that Works: The Case for Balanced Teaching*. New York: Guilford Press.

Prior, M. (1996) *Understanding Specific Learning Difficulties*. Hove: Psychological Press.

Ramjhun, A. (2002) *Implementing the Code of Practice for Children with Special Educational Needs: A Practical Guide* (2nd edn). London: David Fulton Publishers.

Rasinski, T. and Padak, N. (1998) *Effective Reading Strategies: Teaching Children Who Find Reading Difficult* (2nd edn). Upper Saddle River, NJ: Merrill.

Reber, A.S. and Reber, E. (2001) *The Penguin Dictionary of Psychology* (3rd edn). London: Penguin.

Reid, G. (2003) *Dyslexia: A Practitioner's Handbook* (3rd edn). Chichester: Wiley.

Reys, R., Syydam, M., Lindquist, M. and Smith, N. (1998) *Helping Children Learn Mathematics* (5th edn). Boston: Allyn & Bacon.

Richek, M.A., Caldwell, J.S., Jennings, J.H. and Lerner, J.W. (2002) *Reading Problems: Assessment and Teaching Strategies* (4th edn). Boston, MA: Allyn & Bacon.

Riddick, B., Wolf, J. and Lumsdon, D. (2002) *Dyslexia: A Practical Guide for Teachers and Parents*. London: David Fulton Publishers.

Riding, R. (2002) *School Learning and Cognitive Style*. London: David Fulton Publishers.

Ripley, K., Daines, B. and Barrett, J. (1997) *Dyspraxia: A Guide for Teachers and Parents*. London: David Fulton Publishers.

Rose, S., Kamin, L.J. and Lewontin, R.C. (1984) *Not In Our Genes: Biology, Ideology and Human Nature*. London: Penguin.

Rust, J. and Golombuk, S. (1999) *Modern Psychometrics: The Science of Psychological Assessment* (2nd edn). London: Routledge.

Saunders, S. (1999) *Fragile X Syndrome: A Guide for Teachers*. London: David Fulton Publishers.

Schunk, D.H. (2003) *Learning Theories: An Educational Perspective* (3rd edn). Upper Saddle River, NJ: Merrill/ Prentice-Hall.

Selley, N. (1999) *The Art of Constructivist Teaching in Primary School*. London: David Fulton Publishers.

Siegel, L. (1998) 'The discrepancy formula: its use and abuse', in B. Shapiro, P.J. Accardo and A.J. Capute (eds) *Specific Reading Disability: A View of the Spectrum* Timonium, MD: York Press, pp. 121–53.

Silver, A.A. and Hagin, R.A. (2002) *Disorders of Learning in Childhood* (2nd edn). New York: Wiley.

Snell, M.F. and Brown, F. (2000) *Instruction of Students with Severe Disabilities* (5th edn). Upper Saddle River, NJ: Merrill.

Snow, C., Burns, S. and Griffin, P. (1998) *Preventing Reading Difficulties in Young Children*. Washington, DC: National Academy Press.

Stanovich, K.F. (2000) *Progress in Understanding Reading: Scientific Foundations and New Frontiers*. New York: Guilford Press.

Strickland, D.S. (1998) *Teaching Phonics Today: A Primer for Educators*. Newark, DE: International Reading Association.

Stuart, L., Wright, F., Grigor, S. and Howey, A. (2002) *Spoken Language Difficulties: Practical Strategies and Activities for Teachers and Other Professionals*. London: David Fulton Publishers.

Swanson, H.L. (1999) *Interventions for Students with Learning Difficulties: Meta-Analysis of Treatment Outcomes*. New York: Guilford Press.

Talbot, V. (1997) *Teaching Reading, Writing and Spelling*. Thousand Oaks, CA: Corwin Press.

Taly-Ongan, A. (1998) *Typical and Atypical Development in Early Childhood: The Fundamentals*. Leicester: The British Psychological Society.

Thompson, G. (2003) *Supporting Communication Disorders: A Handbook for Teachers and Teaching Assistants*. London: David Fulton Publishers.

Tilstone, C., Lacey, P., Porter, J. and Roberston, C. (2000) *Pupils with Learning Difficulties in Mainstream Schools*. London: David Fulton Publishers.

Tindall, G.A. and Marston, D.B. (1990) *Classroom-Based Assessment*. Columbus, OH: Merrill.

Tod, J. (1999) *IEPs – Dyslexia*. London: David Fulton Publishers.

Tod, J. and Blamires, M. (1998) *IEPs – Speech and Language*. London: David Fulton Publishers.

Topping, K. (1995) *Paired Reading, Spelling and Writing: A Handbook for Teachers and Parents*. London: Cassell.

Turkington, C. and Harris, J. (1992) *The Encyclopedia of Learning Disabilities*. New York: Facts on File.

Turner, A. (2002) *Access to History: Curriculum Planning and Practical Activities for Pupils with Learning Difficulties*. London: David Fulton Publishers.

Tyler, J.S. and Mira, M.P. (1999) *Traumatic Brain Injury in Children and Adolescents: A Sourcebook for Teachers and Other School Personnel* (2nd edn). Austin, TX: ProEd.

Vacca, J.A., Vacca, R.T. and Gove, M.K. (2000). *Reading and Learning to Read* (4th edn). New York: Longman.

Vygotsky, L. (1962) *Thought and Language*. Cambridge, MA: MIT Press.

Walker, B.J. (2000) *Diagnostic Teaching of Reading* (4th edn). Upper Saddle River, NJ: Merrill.

Walker, S. and Wicks, B. (2004) *Educating Children with Acquired Brain Injury*. London: David Fulton Publishers.

Watson, L., Gregory, S. and Powers, S. (1999) *Deaf and Hearing Impaired Pupils in Mainstream Schools*. London: David Fulton Publishers.

Westwood, P. (2004) *Learning and Learning Difficulties: A Handbook for Teachers*. London: David Fulton Publishers.

Westwood, P. (2004) *Numeracy and Learning Difficulties: Approaches to Teaching and Assessment*. London: David Fulton Publishers.

Westwood, P. (2004) *Reading and Learning Difficulties: Approaches to Teaching and Assessment*. London: David Fulton Publishers.

Westwood, P.S. (2003) *Commonsense Methods for Children with Special Needs* (4th edn). London: Routledge-Falmer.

Westwood, P.S. (2004) *Spelling: Approaches to Teaching and Assessment*. London: David Fulton Publishers.

WHO (1992, 1996) *The ICD-10 Classification of Mental and Behavioural Disorders*. Geneva: World Health Organisation.

Wilen, W., Ischler, M., Hutchinson, J. and Kindsvatter, R. (2000) *Dynamics of Effective Teaching* (4th edn). New York: Longmans.

Wing, L. (1996) *The Autistic Spectrum*. London: Constable.

Wolfendale, S. (ed.) (1993) *Assessing Special Educational Needs*. London: Cassell.

Wong, B.Y.L. and Donahue, M.L. (2002) *The Social Dimensions of Learning Disabilities*. Mahwah, NJ: Erlbaum.

Yopp, R.H. and Yopp, H.K. (2001) *Literature-Based Reading Activities* (3rd edn). Boston: Allyn and Bacon.